OXFORD PRIVATE INTERNAT
LAW SERIES

GENERAL EDITOR: JAMES J FAWCETT

Professor of Law
University of Nottingham

THE ANTI-SUIT INJUNCTION

Updating Supplement

OXFORD PRIVATE INTERNATIONAL LAW SERIES

General Editor: James Fawcett

The aim of this series is to publish works of quality and originality in a number of important areas of private international law. The series is intended for both scholarly and practitioner readers.

ALSO IN THIS SERIES

The Rome II Regulation
ANDREW DICKINSON

Intellectual Property and Private International Law (Second Edition)
JAMES J FAWCETT and PAUL TORREMANS

Agreements on Jurisdiction and Choice of Law
ADRIAN BRIGGS

Conflict of Laws Within the UK
KIRSTY J HOOD

Civil Jurisdiction Rules of the EU and their impact on Third States
THALIA KRUGER

Insolvency in Private International Law Main Work (Second Edition) and Supplement
IAN FLETCHER

The Transfer of Property in the Conflict of Laws
JANEEN M CARRUTHERS

International Sale of Goods in the Conflict of Laws
JAMES J FAWCETT, JONATHAN HARRIS, and MICHAEL BRIDGE

Choice of Law for Equitable Doctrines
T M YEO

Procedural Law in International Arbitration
GEORGIOS PETROCHILOS

Foreign Law in Civil Litigation
SOFIE GEEROMS

Cross-Border Divorce Law
MÁIRE NÍ SHÚILLEABHÁIN

Shares and Other Securities in the Conflict of Laws
MAISIE OOI

Forum Shopping and Venue in Transnational Litigation
ANDREW S BELL

Cross-Border Enforcement of Patent Rights
MARTA PERTEGÁS SENDER

Res Judicata, Estoppel, and Foreign Judgments
PETER R BARNETT

Corporations in Private International Law
STEPHAN RAMMELOO

The Enforcement of Judgments in Europe
WENDY KENNETT

Claims for Contribution and Reimbursement in an International Context
KOJI TAKAHASHI

The Hague Convention on International Child Abduction
PAUL BEAUMONT and PETER MCELEAVY

Autonomy in International Contracts
PETER NYGH

Foreign Law in English Courts
RICHARD FENTIMAN

Declining Jurisdiction in Private International Law
JAMES J FAWCETT

THE ANTI-SUIT INJUNCTION

Updating Supplement

THOMAS RAPHAEL

BA (Oxon), BA (Cantab),
of the Middle Temple, Barrister

OXFORD
UNIVERSITY PRESS

OXFORD
UNIVERSITY PRESS

Great Clarendon Street, Oxford OX2 6DP

Oxford University Press is a department of the University of Oxford.
It furthers the University's objective of excellence in research, scholarship,
and education by publishing worldwide in

Oxford New York

Auckland Cape Town Dar es Salaam Hong Kong Karachi
Kuala Lumpur Madrid Melbourne Mexico City Nairobi
New Delhi Shanghai Taipei Toronto

With offices in

Argentina Austria Brazil Chile Czech Republic France Greece
Guatemala Hungary Italy Japan South Korea Poland Portugal
Singapore Switzerland Thailand Turkey Ukraine Vietnam

Oxford is a registered trade mark of Oxford University Press
in the UK and in certain other countries

Published in the United States
by Oxford University Press Inc., New York

Reprinted 2011

ISBN 978-0-19-958847-3

Printed and bound in Great Britain by
CPI Antony Rowe, Chippenham and Eastbourne

Preface to the Updating Supplement

I hope this work has been useful to its readers, who I am glad to say have included the judiciary on a number of occasions.[1] It was, in particular, an honour to have been of assistance to the Court of Appeal in *Deutsche v Highland Crusader Offshore Partners LP*.[2]

When it was written, I had the delicate task of predicting the result of the European Court of Justice's decision in *The Front Comor*.[3] To the relief of the author, if not for the good of English law or the peace of mind of arbitration practitioners, the guesses made turned out roughly to have been right.[4]

But the ramifications of the European Court of Justice's partly surprising reasoning have turned out to be extensive. Together with the reform of CPR Part 6, and the consequences of the House of Lords' third last decision in *Masri v Consolidated Contractors International Ltd (No 4)* [2010] 1 AC 90, considerable parts of the text have required attention.

It is also now clear that the predictions of the death of the anti-suit injunction, made by some in the aftermath of *The Front Comor*, were much exaggerated, and the remedy is instead in rude health. There has been a steady flow of case law combined with a superfluity of academic commentary, and the need to reflect all these developments has merited the production of this supplement.

The aim has been to bring the work up to date to 31 July 2010.

Thomas Raphael
20 Essex Street, London
August 2010

[1] *Sheffield United FC Ltd v West Ham United FC Plc* [2009] 1 Lloyds Rep 167; *National Navigation Co v Endesa Generacion SA (The Wadi Sudr)* [2009] 1 Lloyds Rep 666; *Midgulf International Ltd v Groupe Chimiche Tunisien* [2009] 2 Lloyds Rep 411; *Deutsche Bank AG v Highland Crusader Offshore Partners* [2010] 1 WLR 1023 (CA); *Morgan Stanley & Co International Plc v China Haisheng Juice Holdings Co Ltd* [2010] 1 Lloyds Rep 265; *AES UST-Kamenogorsk Hydropower Plant LLP v UST-Kamenogorsk Hydropower Plant JSC* [2010] EWHC 772 (Comm).

[2] [2010] 1 WLR 1023 (CA), at §§85, 87, 105–106, 112, 126.

[3] *Allianz AG v West Tankers Inc (The Front Comor)* [2009] ECR I-663.

[4] Although it is quite true to say that 'one did not have to be imbued with the soothsaying abilities of an oracle to predict the outcome of the reference': CJS Knight, 'Arbitration and Litigation after *West Tankers*' [2009] LMCLQ 285.

Contents

Tables of Cases

United Kingdom

A v L [2010] EWHC 460 (Fam) 13.36
ABB Lummus Global Ltd v Keppel Fels Ltd [1999] 2 Lloyds Rep 24 . . . . 15.07
Ace Capital Ltd v CMS Energy Corp [2008] 2 CLC 318 . . . . 7.17, 8.04
AES UST-Kamenogorsk Hydropower Plant LLP v UST-Kamenogorsk Hydropower Plant JSC [2010] EWHC 772 (Comm) 3.04, 3.05, 3.14, 7.36, 13.08, 15.04, 15.06, 15.07, 18.26, 18.35, 18.40, 18.41, 18.61
Agbaje v Agbaje [2010] 1 AC 628 (HL) 1.11

Bank of New York Mellon v GV Films [2010] 1 Lloyd's Rep 365 . . . . . 7.21, 8.06, 8.12, 12.11
Barclays Bank Plc v Homan [1993] BCLC 680 . . . . 4.42
Belletti v Morici [2009] ILPr 57 . . . . 3.02, 18.22, 18.59
Bloom v Harms Offshore AHT 'Taurus' & Co Gmbh [2010] Ch 187 (CA) 3.05, 3.06, 3.18, 4.25, 5.28, 5.31, 5.33, 5.35, 7.44
Broda Agro Trade (Cyprus) Limited v Alfred C Toepfer International Gmbh [2010] 1 Lloyds Rep 353 . . . . 11.13

C v D [2008] 1 Lloyds Rep 239 (CA) 7.38
Cecil v Bayat [2010] EWHC 641 . . . . 18.27, 18.28
China Petroleum and Development Corporation v LG Caltex Gas Co Ltd (Unreported, 5 December 2000) 11.09
City & Country Properties Ltd v Kamali [2007] 1 WLR 1219 (CA) 18.04
CMA CGM v Hyundai MIPO Dockyard Co Ltd [2009] 1 Lloyds Rep 213 . . . . 12.26, 12.41, 14.01, 14.11, 14.22, 15.11
Congentra AG v Sixteen Thirteen Marine SA (The Nicholas M) [2008] 2 Lloyds Rep 602 . . . . 4.23, 14.17
Continental Bank v Aeakos Compania Naviera SA [1994] 1 Lloyds Rep 505 (CA) 15.09
Courtman v Ludlam [2009] EWHC 2067 . . . . 6.19

Dallah Estate and Tourism Holding Company v Ministry of Religious Affairs of the Government of Pakistan [2010] 2 WLR 805 (CA) 5.54, 11.24

Foreign Cases

France

Tables of European Cases

European Court of Justice

Alphabetical

Numerical

Table of UK Statutory Instruments

Table of the Brussels-Lugano Regime

Table of International Treaties and Conventions

Table of UK Statutes

1

Introduction

FN 2. The idea that there is a conflict of philosophy between the common law, and a civil law approach, hostile to anti-suit injunctions, requires rethinking in the light of recent developments in the French and German courts: **1.02**

(a) In the case of *In Zone Brands International Inc v In Beverage International*, Cass 1re civ, 14 October 2009, No 08-16.369 and No 08-16.549, the French Cour de Cassation upheld the enforcement in France of an American anti-suit injunction to enforce an exclusive jurisdiction clause and rejected arguments that anti-suit injunctions were an infringement of French judicial sovereignty or an interference with a party's right of access to a court. It may be that there has been a shift in 'civilian' thinking towards a greater sympathy towards the anti-suit injunction.

See T Raphael, 'The Execution of the Anti-Suit Injunction', <http://conflictoflaws.net/2009/the-execution-of-the-anti-suit-injunction/>; H Muir-Watt, 'Surprise? Yes and No', at <http://conflictoflaws.net/2009/ surprise-yes-and-no/>; L Perreau-Saussine, 'Forum conveniens and anti-suit injunctions before French courts: recent developments' (2010) 59 ICLQ 519; and JDI 2010, p 146, Note S Clavel.

(b) In *Vivendi v Gerard*, Cour d'Appel de Paris, 28 April 2010, No 10/01643, the Paris Court of Appeal rejected an appeal against the refusal by the Tribunal de Grande Instance ('TGI') to grant an anti-suit injunction restraining the continuance of proceedings in the USA. However, although it had been argued that French courts did not have power or jurisdiction to grant such injunctions, the Court of Appeal (like the

TGI before it) did not adopt that reasoning, instead rejecting the injunction on the grounds that the USA was a natural forum for the substantive litigation, that there was no illegitimate 'forum shopping', and that the necessary 'fraude' (which can perhaps be best translated as wrongfulness, or even vexation) was not made out on the facts. The Court of Appeal abstained from commenting on the question of power or jurisdiction. The similarity of the reasoning used to that which would be deployed by an English court is striking. See for comment G Cuniberti, 'Abusive Forum Shopping', at <http://conflictoflaws.net/2010/abusive-forum-shopping/>.

(c) The Oberlandesgericht (Dusseldorf) has rejected an application for an anti-suit injunction to restrain the pursuit of proceedings before the German Cartel Office. However, it accepted that such a power existed in principle, and rejected the injunction because the necessary 'special need for legal relief' by way of a preventative measure had not been made out. See I Klass, 'Case Comment: Oberlandesgericht (Dusseldorf) (DFL) (VI-Kart 1/09 (V)' [2010] ECLR N42–43.

A. TERMINOLOGY AND CHARACTERIZATION

1.05 FN 9. See also *Tattersall v Groote* (1800) 2 Bos & P 131, 126 ER 1197 (and the cases there discussed).

1.06 Even the French Cour de Cassation now refers to 'une injonction, dite "anti suit".' See *In Zone Brands International Inc v In Beverage International*, Cass 1re civ, 14 October 2009, No 08-16.369 and No 08-16.549.

B. THE LANDSCAPE OF THE REMEDY

1.09 FN 30. However, for a recent example of an anti-suit injunction to restrain foreign court proceedings see *Sheffield United Football Club Ltd v West Ham United Football Club Plc* [2009] 1 Lloyds Rep 741.

1.10 The European Court's campaign against the anti-suit injunction had been continued, perhaps injudiciously, in *Allianz AG v West Tankers Inc (The Front Comor)* [2009] ECR I-663. See further Ch 12 of this Supplement.

C. ANTI-SUIT INJUNCTIONS AND COMITY

FNs 35 and 38. See *Agbaje v Agbaje* [2010] 1 AC 628 (HL), §§52–53. **1.11**

FN 54. Since *Allianz AG v West Tankers Inc (The Front Comor)* [2009] ECR I-663, there have been some further, if half-hearted, attempts to argue that European law should be applied by analogy to preclude the grant of anti-suit injunctions in respect of proceedings before non-European courts, but they have not got very far: see eg *Midgulf International Ltd v Group Chimique Tunisien* [2009] 2 Lloyd's Rep 411, §§66–69. See further Ch 12 of this Supplement. **1.15**

FN 61. In *Allianz AG v West Tankers Inc (The Front Comor)* [2009] ECR I-663, §28, the European Court of Justice was firmly of the view that an anti-suit injunction was an unacceptable interference with the Regulation jurisdiction of another member state: **1.16**

> the use of an anti-suit injunction to prevent a court of a member state, which normally has jurisdiction to resolve a dispute under Article 5(3) of Regulation 44/2001, from ruling, in accordance with Article 1(2)(d) of that Regulation, on the very applicability of the Regulation to the dispute brought before it necessarily amounts to stripping that court of the power to rule on its own jurisdiction under Regulation 44/2001.

But the view of the English courts (see eg *Midgulf International Ltd v Group Chimique Tunisien* [2009] 2 Lloyd's Rep 411) is that the interference is only unacceptable within the closed sphere of the Brussels–Lugano regime.

No offence was recently taken by the French courts to an American injunction restraining proceedings in France, which was granted to enforce an American exclusive jurisdiction clause: see *In Zone Brands International Inc v In Beverage International*, Cass 1re civ, 14 October 2009, No 08-16.369 and No 08-16.549. However, see §1.24 of this Supplement below. **1.18**

FN 71. This was the objection of Advocate General Kokott in *Allianz AG v West Tankers Inc (The Front Comor)* [2009] ECR I-663, AG §72. **1.19**

FN 78. See the comment at §1.02, FN 2, of this Supplement. **1.21**

FNs 79–80. Arguments based on these principles were advanced before, but rejected by, the French courts: see *In Zone Brands International Inc v In Beverage International*, Cass 1re civ, 14 October 2009, No 08-16.369 and No 08-16.549.

FN 94. It appears to have been the fact that an American anti-suit injunction was enforcing an American exclusive jurisdiction clause, which imposed concrete personal obligations on the injunction defendant, which justified **1.24** the Cour de Cassation's recent willingness to accept the legitimacy of an American anti-suit injunction: *In Zone Brands International Inc v In Beverage International*, Cass 1re civ, 14 October 2009, No 08-16.369 and No 08-16.549. The Cour de Cassation's reasoning suggests that a non-contractual anti-suit injunction might well have encountered considerably greater difficulties.

1.25 FN 95. For an example of the English court accepting the legitimacy of a foreign anti-suit injunction restraining proceedings in England, see *Winnetka Trading Corpn v Julius Baer International Ltd* [2009] Bus LR 1006.

1.26 FN 97. The Advocate General in *The Front Comor* concluded negatively that the proscription of anti-suit injunctions to enforce arbitration clauses within the Brussels–Lugano zone was not itself inconsistent with the New York Convention. There are also aspects of the European Court of Justice's reasoning in that case which could be read as implying that the grant of anti-suit injunctions would be positively inconsistent with the New York Convention: see *Allianz AG v West Tankers Inc (The Front Comor)* [2009] ECR I-663, AG §§55–56, 68; ECJ §33. But there was no clear decision to the latter effect, and the English courts have rejected any such contention: *Midgulf International Ltd v Group Chimique Tunisien* [2009] 2 Lloyd's Rep 411, §§66–69.

1.32 FN 123. For discussion of recent developments in the US case law, see C Lamm, E Hellbeck, J Brubaker, 'Anti-Suit Injunctions in aid of international arbitration: the American approach' (2009) 12 Int ALR 115.

D. HUMAN RIGHTS LAW

1.36 Arguments that an anti-suit injunction, granted by the Superior Court of Cobb County in the State of Georgia, USA, to enforce an exclusive jurisdiction clause in favour of the courts of the State of Georgia, was contrary to the right of access to a court contained in Article 6 of the ECHR were rejected by the French Cour de Cassation: *In Zone Brands International Inc v In Beverage International*, Cass 1re civ, 14 October 2009, No 08-16.369 and No 08-16.549. The Cour de Cassation concluded, in loose translation:

> that there could not be any deprivation of the right of access to a court, in a case where the decision taken by the Georgian judge was, specifically, taken in order to rule on his own jurisdiction, and with an eye on finality, in order to enforce the exclusive jurisdiction clause to which the parties had agreed.

On the other hand, in *Allianz AG v West Tankers Inc (The Front Comor)* [2009] ECR I-663, AG §58, AG Kokott supported the conclusion that anti-suit injunctions were unjustifiable infringements of the right of access to a court. But the European Court of Justice did not adopt this part of her reasoning. See, in support of AG Kokott's approach, K Lenaerts, 'The Contribution of the European Court of Justice to the area of freedom, security and justice' (2010) 59 ICLQ 255, 285–288.

See *In Zone Brands International Inc v In Beverage International*, Cass 1re civ, 14 October 2009, No 08-16.369 and No 08-16.549, discussed at §1.36 of this Supplement, where the French Cour de Cassation adopted reasoning similar to that deployed by Aikens J. **1.41**

E. CONFLICT WITH PUBLIC INTERNATIONAL LAW

See *In Zone Brands International Inc v In Beverage International*, Cass 1re civ, 14 October 2009, No 08-16.369 and No 08-16.549, where the French Cour de Cassation concluded that an anti-suit injunction to enforce an exclusive jurisdiction clause was not contrary to public international law, outside the field of operation of international conventions or EC law. **1.48**

2

The History of an Unusual Remedy

B. THE COURT OF CHANCERY

For further discussion of the history of the common injunction, and the anti-suit injunction's development from it, see D Altaras, 'The anti-suit injunction: historical overview' (2009) 75 Arbitration 327. **2.02**

G. *TURNER V GROVIT*

Lord Goff's test of vexation and oppression appears to be gaining the upper hand. See *Deutsche Bank AG v Highland Crusader Offshore Partners* [2010] 1 WLR 1023 (CA), §50; *Elektrim SA v Vivendi Holdings 1 Corporation* [2009] 1 Lloyds Rep 59 (CA), §82. **2.19**

FNs 82 and 83. The European Court has followed *Turner v Grovit* with its decision in *Allianz AG v West Tankers Inc (The Front Comor)* [2009] ECR I-663, where it held that anti-suit injunctions to enforce an arbitration clause were also precluded by the Brussels–Lugano regime where they sought to restrain proceedings before another Brussels–Lugano court within the material scope of the Brussels–Lugano regime. **2.20**

Nevertheless, the contention that the European Court's approach should be transferred to preclude injunctions in respect of proceedings outside the Brussels–Lugano zone has been rejected by the English courts: *Shashoua v Sharma* [2009] 2 Lloyds Rep 376, §§35–39; *Midgulf International Ltd v Groupe Chimiche Tunisien* [2009] 2 Lloyd's Rep 411, §§67–68.

3

Power, Nature, and Form

B. THE POWER TO GRANT INJUNCTIONS

The same conceptual distinction, expressed as being between 'substantive jurisdiction' and 'territorial jurisdiction', rather than 'power' and 'jurisdiction', was deployed in *Belletti v Morici* [2009] ILPr 57, §44. **3.02**

FN 7. The Constitutional Reform Act 2005 is now in force and we now have a Supreme Court. **3.03**

FN 8. The Supreme Court Act 1981 is now named the Senior Courts Act 1981 following the coming into force of the Constitutional Reform Act 2005 on 1 October 2009.

FN 14. In confirmation of the self-evident proposition that contractual injunctions enforce a legal or equitable right, see *AES UST-Kamenogorsk Hydropower Plant LLP v UST-Kamenogorsk Hydropower Plant JSC* [2010] EWHC 772 (Comm), §19(iii), 20. **3.04**

FN 17. *Fourie v Le Roux* was also cited in *Secretary of State for the Environment, Food and Rural Affairs v Meier* [2009] 1 WLR 2780 (HL), §97. However, it was not cited in *AES UST-Kamenogorsk Hydropower Plant LLP v UST-Kamenogorsk Hydropower Plant JSC* [2010] EWHC 772 (Comm), §§18–20, and thus Burton J's approach to *The Siskina* is unsound, although this did not affect the result. *Fourie v Le Roux* was also surprisingly not cited in *L'Oreal SA v eBay International AG* [2009] ETMR 53, §§447–454, where Arnold J nevertheless felt willing to tiptoe beyond the boundaries of *The Siskina*.

FN 18. The established proposition that the statutory prohibitions arising on winding up against litigation against company in liquidation do not **3.05** apply to proceedings outside the United Kingdom was extended, by parity of reasoning, to the analogous provisions in relation to administration: *Bloom v Harms Offshore AHT 'Taurus' & Co Gmbh* [2010] Ch 187 (CA), §16.

FN 19. In *Hospira UK Ltd v Eli Lilly & Company* [2008] EWHC 1862 (Pat), Floyd J *obiter* considered that the basis of the power to restrain proceedings in England was the inherent jurisdiction of the court. But it is submitted that the analysis in the text of this work should be preferred. Floyd J's reasoning confuses anti-suit injunctions, which restrain vexatious proceedings, and orders to restrain vexatious litigants, which are a different matter: see Ch 6, §6.19.

FN 20. See also *AES UST-Kamenogorsk Hydropower Plant LLP v UST-Kamenogorsk Hydropower Plant JSC* [2010] EWHC 772 (Comm), §§19–20, holding that section 37(1) of the Senior Courts Act 1981 could support the grant of a final anti-suit injunction to enforce an arbitration clause, even where no arbitration had actually been commenced nor was one likely to be commenced. In contrast, section 44 of the Arbitration Act 1996 could not support the grant of a final anti-suit injunction: §§18(i), 20.

3.06 FN 22. For other examples of injunctions to restrain ship arrest proceedings, see *Kallang Shipping SA Panama v Axa Assurances Senegal (The Kallang) (No 2)* [2009] 1 Lloyds Rep 124; *Sotrade Denizcilik Sanayi Ve Ticaret AS v Amadou Lo (The Duden)* [2009] 1 Lloyds Rep 145.

In *Bloom v Harms Offshore AHT 'Taurus' & Co Gmbh* [2010] Ch 187 (CA), a mandatory injunction was granted requiring the injunction defendant to discharge a Rule B attachment obtained in New York.

3.07 FN 23. In the case of *In Zone Brands International Inc v In Beverage International*, Cass 1re civ, 14 October 2009, No 08-16.369 and No 08-16.549 (see JDI 2010, p 146, Note S Clavel), the French Cour de Cassation concluded that the grant of *exequatur* to an American anti-suit injunction enforcing an exclusive jurisdiction clause in favour of the Courts of Georgia did not restrict the right of access to a court.

C. A LEGAL OR EQUITABLE RIGHT?

3.08 FN 24. *Kallang Shipping SA Panama v Axa Assurances Senegal (The Kallang) (No 2)* [2009] 1 Lloyds Rep 124, was the trial of the action in *The Kallang*. Axa Senegal, who were the insurers of the cargo receivers, and who had controlled legal proceedings in Senegal brought in breach of the arbitration clause by the cargo receivers against the shipowners, with the aim of forcing the shipowners to give up their right to arbitrate in London and instead to accept Senegalese jurisdiction, were held liable in damages for wrongful inducement of the cargo receivers' breach (§§90–94). The same result was reached in *Sotrade Denizcilik Sanayi Ve Ticaret AS v Amadou Lo (The Duden)* [2009] 1 Lloyds Rep 145, §§65–68. However, Jonathan Hirst QC stressed in both decisions that both parties agreed that this issue was to be decided in accordance with English law, and that no case on Senegalese law was pleaded (§90). If the applicable law point had been taken, the result might well have been different: see Ch 14, §14.18 of the original text.

The learned Deputy Judge also held alternative claims for interference with contract by unlawful means added nothing (§94) and rejected a claim for conspiracy on the facts (§96).

A Briggs, *Agreements on Jurisdiction and Choice of Law* (OUP, 2008), §6.26, supports the proposition that general non-contractual anti-suit injunctions are based on an 'ordinary civil wrong', whether tortious or equitable. **3.10**

D. THE FORM AND NATURE OF FINAL ANTI-SUIT INJUNCTIONS

FN 45. The conclusion in the first paragraph of the footnote was adopted in *AES UST-Kamenogorsk Hydropower Plant LLP v UST-Kamenogorsk Hydropower Plant JSC* [2010] EWHC 772 (Comm). **3.14**

The proposition in the main text, and in the second paragraph of the footnote, has also been supported by the authorities.

(a) A permanent anti-suit injunction to enforce an arbitration clause was sought by claim form in *Steamship Mutual Underwriting Association (Bermuda) Ltd v Sulpicio Lines Inc* [2008] 2 Lloyds Rep 269, §§10, 28, and was granted.

(b) In *AES UST-Kamenogorsk Hydropower Plant LLP v UST-Kamenogorsk Hydropower Plant JSC* [2010] EWHC 772 (Comm), arbitration proceedings had not been commenced and there was no apparent intention to commence them. The defendant commenced proceedings in Kazakhstan and the claimant sought, by arbitration claim form, a final declaration that the arbitration clause was binding and a final injunction restraining the Kazakhstan proceedings. The claimant's ability to use an arbitration claim for this purpose was disputed by the defendant on the grounds that there was no existing or likely arbitration, but Burton J accepted that an arbitration claim form could validly be used for this purpose: §§19(vi), 20. This is correct: a claim to declare the validity of an arbitration agreement is within CPR 62.2(1)(b); and a claim to enforce it by injunction is probably an 'application . . . affecting . . . an arbitration agreement' within rule 62.2(d)(ii). Burton J also concluded that the fact that the standard form arbitration claim form included the heading 'In the matter of an [intended] arbitration' did not require that an arbitration had been or was intended to be commenced: at §§18(viii), 19(vii), 23. However, Burton J did not need to consider whether such final injunctions should *only* be sought by arbitration claim form.

As to the third paragraph of the footnote, in C-185/07, *West Tankers Inc v Ras Riunione di Sicurta (The Front Comor)* [2009] 1 AC 1138 (ECJ), §23, the European Court of Justice agreed with Lord Hoffmann that an anti-suit injunction to enforce an arbitration clause was 'arbitration' for the purposes of the arbitration exception. The European Court's disagreement with Lord Hoffmann on the separate question of whether, notwithstanding this, the grant of an anti-suit injunction to restrain proceedings in another member state was precluded by the principle of mutual trust does not affect the argument in the footnote.

3.16 FN 51. However, in *Skype Technologies SA v Joltid* [2009] EWHC 2783 (Ch), §41, Lewison J treated the inclusion of a 'liberty to apply' as creating a general discretionary power to permit subsequent proceedings abroad on application by the injunction defendant.

3.18 FN 56. See also *Kallang Shipping SA Panama v Axa Assurances Senegal (The Kallang) (No 2)* [2009] 1 Lloyds Rep 124, §§25–32, and *Sotrade Denizcilik Sanayi Ve Ticaret AS v Amadou Lo (The Duden)* [2009] 1 Lloyds Rep 145, §23.

FN 57. In *Bloom v Harms Offshore AHT 'Taurus' & Co Gmbh* [2010] 2 WLR 349 (CA), a mandatory injunction was granted requiring the injunction defendant to discharge a Rule B attachment obtained in New York.

FN 58. For further old authority against the proposition that arbitration agreements can be specifically enforced, see *Tattersall v Groote* (1800) 2 Bos & P 131, 126 ER 1197.

FN 58. Following the European Court of Justice's conclusion in *West Tankers Inc v Ras Riunione di Sicurta (The Front Comor)* [2009] 1 AC 1138 (ECJ), §23 (where it was held that prohibitory injunctions restraining parties from litigating in breach of an arbitration clause before the courts of other member states are inconsistent with the Brussels–Lugano regime), there may be pressure to re-examine the proposition that mandatory injunctions, or specific performance, should not be granted positively to require a party to arbitrate (or litigate) before a particular forum. There would, however, be reason to doubt whether this stratagem could evade the effect of the principle of mutual trust as understood by the European Court of Justice.

E. AGAINST WHOM MAY AN ANTI-SUIT INJUNCTION BE GRANTED?

FN 67. For other examples of anti-suit injunctions being brought against third parties who have induced or procured a contractual counterparty to breach an arbitration clause, see *Kallang Shipping SA Panama v Axa Assurances Senegal (The Kallang) (No 2)* [2009] 1 Lloyds Rep 124; *Sotrade Denizcilik Sanayi Ve Ticaret AS v Amadou Lo (The Duden)* [2009] 1 Lloyds Rep 145. **3.21**

FN 69. In *Sotrade Denizcilik Sanayi Ve Ticaret AS v Amadou Lo (The Duden)* [2009] 1 Lloyds Rep 145, the injunction defendants were at one stage in breach of a without notice anti-suit injunction, restraining proceedings before the courts of Senegal. Applications were made for contempt and to join the injunction defendants' French avocats (who had offices in London) to the proceedings as defendants. In *obiter* and *extempore* oral comments during the course of a hearing, Morison J suggested that there were 'good grounds for joining the French solicitors who also appear to be in contempt' (§27). But it seems that Morison J's attention was not drawn to the previous authorities.

It is submitted that it is inconsistent with comity to seek to bring contempt proceedings against foreign lawyers directly in respect of the conduct of foreign proceedings. They will in most cases be doing no more than complying with their professional duties to do their best for their client within the framework of their own legal system. To move beyond the client to the lawyer will usually be an infringement of the personal logic of the anti-suit injunction. One specific feature of *The Duden* was that the French avocats had, in the judge's view, mistated the nature of the anti-suit injunction to the Senegalese judge by suggesting in oral argument before him that 'the English court holds him in contempt' (§26).

4

Injunctions to Restrain Proceedings Abroad: General Principles

A. THE GENERAL PRINCIPLES

Summaries of the law consistent with that formulated in the main text were deployed by the Court of Appeal in *Elektrim SA v Vivendi Holdings 1 Corporation* [2009] 1 Lloyds Rep 59 (CA), §82 and *Deutsche Bank AG v Highland Crusader Offshore Partners* [2010] 1 WLR 1023 (CA), §50. **4.01**

B. APPLICABLE LAW

The Rome II Regulation is now in force. **4.06–4.09**

FN 13. See also *OJSC Oil Company Yugraneft v Abramovich* [2008] EWHC 2613 (Comm), §§170–223. **4.06**

C. A DISCRETIONARY REMEDY GOVERNED BY PRINCIPLE

4.10 See *Deutsche Bank AG v Highland Crusader Offshore Partners* [2010] 1 WLR 1023 (CA), §50(8).

D. THE ENDS OF JUSTICE

4.11 See *Deutsche Bank AG v Highland Crusader Offshore Partners* [2010] 1 WLR 1023 (CA), §50.

E. UNCONSCIONABLE CONDUCT

4.15 For a recent example of a lucid summary of the law which does not incorporate the concept of unconscionability, see *Deutsche Bank AG v Highland Crusader Offshore Partners* [2010] 1 WLR 1023 (CA), §50. The concepts of vexation or oppression were employed in *Elektrim SA v Vivendi Holdings 1 Corporation* [2009] 1 Lloyds Rep 59 (CA), §82.

F. A LEGAL OR EQUITABLE RIGHT

4.23 FN 74. The rule that the foreign proceedings must have failed in order for the tort of maliciously procuring the commencement of civil proceedings to be made out, applies only to substantive foreign proceedings which involve an examination of the factual merits, and not to ex parte applications or attachments: *Congentra AG v Sixteen Thirteen Marine SA (The Nicholas M)* [2008] 2 Lloyds Rep 602, §§38–44.

FN 77. In *Land Securities Ltd v Fladgate Fielder* [2010] 2 WLR 1265, the Court of Appeal held that there was no general tort of abuse of civil process, but only defined and limited instances of liability. However for a slightly more flexible approach, recognizing the possibility of a tort of wrongful attachment and of incremental development of the categories of liability, see *Congentra AG v Sixteen Thirteen Marine SA (The Nicholas M)* [2008] 2 Lloyds Rep 602, §§20–23.

FNs 79 and 81. The conflict of laws provisions of the Private International Law (Miscellaneous Provisions) Act 1995 have now been replaced by the Rome II Regulation, with effect from 11 January 2009. **4.24**

FN 80. In *Kallang Shipping SA Panama v Axa Assurances Senegal (The Kallang) (No 2)* [2009] 1 Lloyds Rep 124 (§§90–94) and *Sotrade Denizcilik Sanayi Ve Ticaret AS v Amadou Lo (The Duden)* [2009] 1 Lloyds Rep 145 (§§65–68), English law was applied to tortious claims against the insurer of a party to an arbitration clause when the insurer had induced his insured to breach the arbitration clause by bringing proceedings in Senegal. But as the judge was at pains to point out, neither party argued that Senegalese law should apply and there was no evidence of Senegalese law.

See now *Kallang Shipping SA Panama v Axa Assurances Senegal (The Kallang) (No 2)* [2009] 1 Lloyds Rep 124 (§§90–94) and *Sotrade Denizcilik Sanayi Ve Ticaret AS v Amadou Lo (The Duden)* [2009] 1 Lloyds Rep 145 (§§65–68), where damages were awarded in tort for inducement of a breach of contract against an insurer who had orchestrated his insured's breaches of an arbitration clause. However, choice of law problems were not addressed. **4.25**

FN 92. Professor Briggs' criticisms of *Samengo-Turner* have also been expressed in his book, *Agreements on Jurisdiction and Choice of Law* (OUP, 2008), §§3.46–3.47. **4.26**

G. VEXATIOUS OR OPPRESSIVE CONDUCT

FN 99. See recently *Deutsche Bank AG v Highland Crusader Offshore Partners* [2010] 1 WLR 1023 (CA), §50(2). **4.28**

FN 100. It is a necessary condition of a valid cause of action for a final anti-suit injunction on a quia timet basis that the injunction defendant must be, at least, threatening or intending to bring the allegedly wrongful proceedings: *Hospira UK Ltd v Eli Lilly & Company* [2008] EWHC 1862 (Pat), §§511–13.

FN 104. 'The categories of factors which indicate vexation and oppression are not closed': *Elektrim SA v Vivendi Holdings 1 Corporation* [2009] 1 Lloyds Rep 59 (CA), §83.

FN 107. See recently *Elektrim SA v Vivendi Holdings 1 Corporation* [2009] 1 Lloyds Rep 59 (CA), §83. **4.29**

H. INTERFERENCE WITH THE PROCESS OF THE ENGLISH COURT

4.34 An injunction was justified to protect the jurisdiction of the English court in *Elektrim SA v Vivendi Holdings 1 Corporation* [2009] 1 Lloyds Rep 59 (CA), §§159–160, where the foreign proceedings were a collateral attack on a prior English judgment, and the claims therein could and should have been raised in the prior English litigation.

I. *FORUM NON CONVENIENS*

4.36 FN 138. See also *Deutsche Bank AG v Highland Crusader Offshore Partners* [2010] 1 WLR 1023 (CA), §§50, 54.

J. LEGITIMATE AND ILLEGITIMATE ADVANTAGES

4.37 The absence of any perceived legitimate advantage in pursuing the foreign proceedings does not automatically mean that the injunction should be granted, 'for that would be to overlook the important restraining influence of considerations of comity': *Deutsche Bank AG v Highland Crusader Offshore Partners* [2010] 1 WLR 1023 (CA), §50(4).

K. COMITY

4.40 See *Deutsche Bank AG v Highland Crusader Offshore Partners* [2010] 1 WLR 1023 (CA), §50.

4.41 FN 153. See also *Deutsche Bank AG v Highland Crusader Offshore Partners* [2010] 1 WLR 1023 (CA), §56.

FN 154. See *Deutsche Bank AG v Highland Crusader Offshore Partners* [2010] 1 WLR 1023 (CA), §50(5): in non-contractual cases

> the principle of comity requires the court to recognize that, in deciding questions of weight to be attached to different factors, different judges operating under different legal systems with different legal policies may legitimately arrive at different answers, without occasioning a breach of customary international law or manifest injustice, and that in such circumstances it is not for an English court to arrogate to itself the decision how a foreign court should determine the matter.

FN 161. In *Deutsche Bank AG v Highland Crusader Offshore Partners* [2010] 1 WLR 1023 (CA), §56, the Court of Appeal applied *Re Maxwell* (referred to in the main text under the name *Barclays Bank v Homan*), and concluded: **4.42**

where the court is not enforcing a contractual right under English law, the normal assumption is that an English court has no superiority over a foreign court in deciding what justice between the parties requires and, in particular, that both comity and common sense suggest that the foreign judge is usually the best person to decide whether in his own court he should accept or decline jurisdiction, stay proceedings or allow them to continue. In other words, there must be good reason why the decision to stop the foreign proceedings should be made by an English judge rather than a foreign judge, and cases where justice requires the English court to intervene will be exceptional.

See also §§50, 119–120.

FN 171. It can be noted, however, that the French courts have recently agreed to enforce an American anti-suit injunction: *In Zone Brands International Inc v In Beverage International*, Cass 1re civ, 14 October 2009, No 08-16.369 and No 08-16.549. **4.45**

The common law rules as to service out of the jurisdiction are now contained in new CPR Part 6 Section IV. **4.46**

See *Deutsche Bank AG v Highland Crusader Offshore Partners* [2010] 1 WLR 1023 (CA), §56. **4.49**

M. OTHER DISCRETIONARY CONSIDERATIONS

FN 206. An application for an anti-suit injunction was held to have been brought prematurely, and therefore refused, in *Hospira UK Ltd v Eli Lilly & Company* [2008] EWHC 1862 (Pat), §§11–13, where the defendant had not actually threatened to bring proceedings, but had merely reserved its rights to do so. **4.55**

5

Non-Contractual Anti-Suit Injunctions

B. ALTERNATIVE FORUM CASES

FN 7. See also *Deutsche Bank AG v Highland Crusader Offshore Partners* [2010] 1 WLR 1023 (CA), §§50(6), 63, 119. **5.03**

FN 10. See also *Deutsche Bank AG v Highland Crusader Offshore Partners* [2010] 1 WLR 1023 (CA), §§50(5)–(6), 63, 117–119. **5.04**

FN 23. For a further example of a case holding that a criticism of the quality of justice in a foreign court 'should not be made and will be rejected unless there is a clear evidence to support it', see *Middle Eastern Oil v National Bank of Abu Dhabi* [2008] 2 CLC 1026, §§22–27. See also *Agbaje v Agbaje* [2010] 1 AC 628 (HL), §53. **5.07**

FN 26. See also *Deutsche Bank AG v Highland Crusader Offshore Partners* [2010] 1 WLR 1023 (CA), §50(5). **5.08**

C. INJUNCTIONS TO PREVENT RELITIGATION

FN 49. In *Elektrim SA v Vivendi Holdings 1 Corporation* [2009] 1 Lloyds Rep 59 (CA), §85, Lawrence Collins LJ treated his earlier judgment in *Masri v Consolidated Contractors International Co SAL (No 3)* [2009] QB 503 (CA) as correctly stating the law. **5.15**

5.15–5.16 For discussion, see A Briggs, 'Enforcing and reinforcing an English judgment' [2008] LMCLQ 421.

5.17 In *Elektrim SA v Vivendi Holdings 1 Corporation* [2009] 1 Lloyds Rep 59 (CA), §§159–160, an injunction was ordered to 'protect the jurisdiction of the English court', where the foreign proceedings were an attempt to mount a collateral attack on a prior English judgment, and the claim made could and should have been raised in the earlier English litigation.

D. SINGLE FORUM CASES

5.23 FNs 65–68. In *Elektrim SA v Vivendi Holdings 1 Corporation* [2009] 1 Lloyds Rep 59 (CA), §§84, 111, 120–121, the Court of Appeal observed that:

> An application for an anti-suit injunction should not be used as a means of obtaining a summary determination of the foreign claims in an English court . . . but if there are other factors which indicate vexation or oppression, the weakness of the case on the merits may be a further compelling factor.

However, it may be that weakness of the foreign claim will suffice if the foreign claim is 'utterly absurd': *Elektrim SA v Vivendi Holdings 1 Corporation* [2009] 1 Lloyds Rep 59 (CA), §111.

5.24 FN 68. See *Elektrim SA v Vivendi Holdings 1 Corporation* [2009] 1 Lloyds Rep 59 (CA), §§84, 120–121, where Lawrence Collins LJ took a similar, although perhaps slightly more robust line. He concluded that:

> In considering whether a cause of action in a foreign country is vexatious or oppressive on the grounds that it is bound to fail, the English judge should not conduct a summary determination under English law principles without regard to the fact that the foreign law system of pleadings may be more liberal, or that the foreign system of discovery may yield sufficient material to support allegations. . . but the inherent weakness of a claim, taken together with other matters, may be an important factor in the consideration of whether foreign proceedings are vexatious or oppressive.

5.28 FN 80. See now *Bloom v Harms Offshore AHT 'Taurus' & Co Gmbh* [2010] Ch 187 (CA).

E. INSOLVENCY AND JUSTICE BETWEEN CREDITORS

5.31 FN 87. Injunctions can also be granted to prevent English administration proceedings: *Bloom v Harms Offshore AHT 'Taurus' & Co Gmbh* [2010] Ch 187 (CA), §24.

FN 93. See, for example, *Bloom v Harms Offshore AHT 'Taurus' & Co Gmbh* [2010] Ch 187 (CA), §§27–29, where the recalcitrant creditors had laid a 'trap' for the administrators by undisclosed Rule B attachments in New York which then captured dollar payments being made by the administrators. Injunctions to protect insolvencies or administrations can also be justified on the grounds of protecting the jurisdiction of the English court: see §26. **5.33**

FN 99. In *Bloom v Harms Offshore AHT 'Taurus' & Co Gmbh* [2010] 2 WLR 349 (CA), §29, the Court of Appeal concluded that 'the conduct of the creditor companies and the circumstances of the attachments brought it into the exceptional category in which the grant of injunctive relief is justified, notwithstanding comity'. It was particularly relevant that there was nothing connecting the facts of the case, or the creditors, to the United States, where the attachment proceedings were brought: §28. **5.35**

F. STAY APPLICATIONS IN THE FOREIGN COURT

FN 114. In *Deutsche Bank AG v Highland Crusader Offshore Partners* [2010] 1 WLR 1023 (CA), the Texas judge had dismissed an application for a stay after having heard argument based on principles akin to *forum non conveniens*. His decision was a powerful reason against the grant of a non-contractual anti-suit injunction by the English court: at §119. **5.40**

FN 115. In *Deutsche Bank AG v Highland Crusader Offshore Partners* [2010] 1 WLR 1023 (CA), the Court of Appeal referred to the possibility that

> there may be exceptional circumstances where the interests of justice, as perceived by the English court, require the grant of an injunction to restrain foreign proceedings which the foreign court considers it proper to entertain

but concluded that the case before them was not such a case.

H. ANTI-ANTI-SUIT INJUNCTIONS

FN 133. In *Winnetka Trading Corpn v Julius Baer International Ltd* [2009] Bus LR 1006, §12, it was treated as obvious that the fact that English proceedings were in breach of a foreign anti-suit injunction, and were thus a contempt of the foreign court's order, did not mean the English court should refuse to hear the person restrained by the foreign court's order. **5.47**

For an example of the English court accepting the legitimacy of a foreign anti-suit injunction restraining proceedings in England, see *Winnetka* **5.48**

Trading Corpn v Julius Baer International Ltd [2009] Bus LR 1006, where the existence of a Guernsey anti-suit injunction restraining proceedings in England was a powerful factor supporting the grant of a stay of proceedings in England.

5.49 For discussion of the American approach to foreign anti-suit injunctions, see C Lamm, E Hellbeck, J Brubaker, 'Anti-Suit Injunctions in aid of international arbitration: the American approach' (2009) 12 Int ALR 115, 122.

I. ANTI-ENFORCEMENT INJUNCTIONS

5.54 In *Sheltam Rail Co (Pty) Ltd v Mirambo Holdings* [2008] 2 Lloyds Rep 195, the claimant, after having lost an arbitration, had commenced and then sought to discontinue an appeal against the arbitration award under section 67 of the Arbitration Act 1996. The court would have permitted discontinuance only on terms that the claimant undertook, as indeed the claimant did undertake, not to resist enforcement of the award abroad in reliance on arguments that could have been raised in the section 67 proceedings (see §37). It can be questioned whether this interference with the foreign court's ability and right to assess the enforceability of an award is legitimate. When themselves considering whether or not to enforce a foreign arbitration award, the English courts consider themselves at liberty to consider arguments against enforcement which could have been raised before the supervisory court, even if a challenge to the award was commenced before the supervisory court and then 'waived': *Dallah Estate and Tourism Holding Company v Ministry of Religious Affairs of the Government of Pakistan* [2010] 2 WLR 805 (CA), §§56, 61, 90. See further the authorities referred to at §7.22, point (b) of this Supplement.

6

Injunctions in Relation to Proceedings in England and Wales

A. INTRODUCTION

FN 3. A Briggs, *Agreements on Jurisdiction and Choice of Law* (OUP, 2008), §6.08, states categorically that anti-suit injunctions are not granted to restrain proceedings in England, but this is incorrect, as this chapter shows. **6.01**

FNs 5 and 6. In *Hospira UK Ltd v Eli Lilly & Company* [2008] EWHC 1862 (Pat), Floyd J was prepared in principle to restrain potential proceedings in the High Court that had not yet been commenced, although the possible survival, and potential scope, of the rule prohibiting the restraint of 'pending' proceedings in the High Court was not debated. **6.02**

B. POWERS TO GRANT INJUNCTIONS IN RELATION TO ENGLISH PROCEEDINGS

FN 16. In *Hospira UK Ltd v Eli Lilly & Company* [2008] EWHC 1862 (Pat), §12, Floyd J derived the jurisdictional basis of the injunction from the Court's inherent power to protect its proceedings from abuse (at §9), and relied on the authorities relating to vexatious litigants. It is submitted that the better view remains that an injunction to restrain other proceedings finds its modern statutory basis in section 37 of the Supreme Court Act 1981 and its historical juridical basis in equity: see Ch 3, §3.05. **6.04**

The concept of abuse of process is more apt to the stay of proceedings before the court granting the order than the restraint of proceedings before another court, since in the first case there is no 'abuse' of the proceedings of the court granting the injunction: see Ch 4, §4.32 of the original text. Where an anti-suit injunction is granted in respect of other courts of England and Wales, there is an obvious temptation to view the two courts as the same, and thus to assimilate the remedy to the court's control of its own proceedings, but this is a temptation to be resisted, as it leads to confusion.

Further, a clear distinction should be preserved between the restraint of vexatious litigants and the restraint of vexatious proceedings: see Ch 6, §6.19.

FN 19. In *Hospira UK Ltd v Eli Lilly & Company* [2008] EWHC 1862 (Pat), Floyd J was prepared in principle to restrain potential proceedings in the High Court that had not yet been commenced, although the (possible) prohibition by statute of the restraint of 'pending' proceedings in the High Court was not referred to before him.

In *Mentmore Towers Ltd v Packman Lucas Ltd* [2010] BLR 393, injunctions were granted to restrain the pursuit of adjudications under the Housing Grants, Construction and Regeneration Act 1996.

C. PRINCIPLES GOVERNING INJUNCTIONS IN ENGLAND

6.06 FN 24. In *Hospira UK Ltd v Eli Lilly & Company* [2008] EWHC 1862 (Pat), §12, Floyd J applied the threshold concept of vexatiousness.

G. ORDERS TO RESTRAIN VEXATIOUS LITIGANTS

6.19 FN 64. See *Courtman v Ludlam* [2009] EWHC 2067, §§13–14, explaining that although CROs are not *'punishment'* for past conduct, the past is highly relevant to establishing the 'threat level' of the continuation of future unmeritorious litigation.

7

Anti-Suit Injunctions and Exclusive Forum Clauses

B. THE EFFECT OF THE BRUSSELS–LUGANO REGIME

7.05 The European Court of Justice has now concluded that anti-suit injunctions to enforce an arbitration clause by restraining court proceedings in another member state are within the scope of the Brussels I Regulation and contrary to the principle of mutual trust, and consequently are precluded by the Brussels I Regulation: C-185/07, *Allianz Spa v West Tankers Inc (The Front Comor)* [2009] ECR I-663. See further the discussion in this Supplement under Ch 12.

D. THE *ANGELIC GRACE* PRINCIPLES

7.08 FN 10. In *Skype Technologies SA v Joltid* [2009] EWHC 2783 (Ch), §§21–27, Lewison J correctly rejected an argument that if an English court had jurisdiction under Article 23 of the Brussels I Regulation, it was obliged to grant an anti-suit injunction to restrain parallel proceedings abroad in breach of that clause, and had no discretion to refuse the injunction. He also correctly concluded (at §§30–31) that it would be inappropriate to apply the rule in *Doherty v Allman* (1878) 3 App Cas 708 (HL), (namely, that there was no discretion to refuse an injunction to enforce a clear negative covenant) to anti-suit injunctions.

Conversely, in *Elektrim SA v Vivendi Holdings 1 Corporation* [2009] 1 Lloyds Rep 59 (CA), §81, a case concerning a 'no action' clause, it was conceded by the injunction defendant that if the 'no action clause' was applicable, then an injunction was the appropriate remedy 'because the court would ordinarily enforce a negative covenant by injunction'. This concession probably does not reflect the law, in the light of the authorities in §7.08 FN 10 of the original work. Those authorities concern injunctions to enforce exclusive jurisdiction clauses, but it is submitted that the same principle applies to injunctions to enforce 'no action clauses'. The inherent dangers of anti-suit injunctions preclude cross-application of the standard negative covenant rule.

7.09 For a recent example of these principles being applied, see *Transfield Shipping v Chiping Xinfa Huayu Alumina Co Ltd* [2009] EWHC 3629 (QB), §§48, 49.

7.10 FN 26. In *Midgulf International Ltd v Groupe Chimiche Tunisien* [2009] 2 Lloyd's Rep 411, §§67–68, the Court of Appeal reaffirmed the existing doctrine that the grant of an anti-suit injunction was not incompatible with the New York Convention. They concluded that there was nothing in the decision of the European Court of Justice in C-185/07, *Allianz Spa v West Tankers Inc (The Front Comor)* [2009] ECR I-663 which required a different view to be taken. The same conclusion had also been reached, with more extensive reasoning, by Cooke J in *Shashoua v Sharma* [2009] 2 Lloyds Rep 376, §§35–39. See also §1.26 of this Supplement.

Para 3 of footnote. For further discussion of the US approach to the interplay between the New York Convention and anti-suit injunctions, see C Lamm, E Hellbeck, J Brubaker, 'Anti-Suit Injunctions in aid of international arbitration: the American approach' (2009) 12 Int ALR 115.

7.16 See also *Midgulf International Ltd v Groupe Chimiche Tunisien* [2009] 2 Lloyd's Rep 411, §§67–68.

E. THE SCOPE AND LIMITS OF EXCLUSIVE FORUM CLAUSES

7.17 FN 47. In *Ace Capital Ltd v CMS Energy Corp* [2008] 2 CLC 318, the contract combined an English arbitration clause and a US service of suit clause. Christopher Clarke J held the arbitration clause was not qualified by the service of suit clause, so that proceedings on the merits in the US courts were a breach of contract. The clauses could be reconciled, but the function of the service of suit clause was to found US jurisdiction in respect of proceedings before the US courts brought to enforce the arbitration clause or any arbitration award.

Where a bill of lading contains a *Himalaya* clause prohibiting claims against the servants, agents, stevedores or subcontractors of the carrier, and the cargo interests and the subrogated insurers seek to sue such third parties (so as to evade the exclusive jurisdiction clause in the bill of lading), the court can enforce the *Himalaya* clause by anti-suit injunction against the cargo interests and their subrogated insurers at the suit of the carrier: *Whiteseas Shipping and Trading Corporation v El Paso Rio Clara Ltda (The Marielle Bolten)* [2010] 1 Lloyds Rep 648, §21. **7.18**

There is a growing divide in the authorities in relation to whether and on what basis a contractual anti-suit injunction can be obtained against parties to an exclusive forum clause who seek to sue, not their contractual counterparty, but instead a connected third party, in a court which is not the contractually chosen court.

(a) In *Horn Linie GmbH v Panamericana Formas e Impresos SA (The Hornbay)* [2006] 2 Lloyds Rep 44, such an injunction had been granted, but apparently on the basis that it was vexatious and oppressive to seek to evade an exclusive forum clause by suing a connected third party. It is submitted that this is usually the right analysis.

(b) In *Morgan Stanley & Co International Plc v China Haisheng Juice Holdings Co Ltd* [2010] 1 Lloyd's Rep 265, Teare J held that on its true construction the exclusive jurisdiction clause before him did not prohibit proceedings against a connected third party who was not party to the agreement, even where they arose out of the same commercial relationship covered by the agreement (not following comments made by Lord Scott in *Donohue v Armco* [2002] 1 Lloyds Rep 425, §§60–61).

(c) In contrast, in *Vitol SA v Arcturus Merchant Trust Ltd* [2009] Bus LR 271, §36, Blair J held (following *The Hornbay* as he interpreted it), that it was a *breach* of the exclusive jurisdiction clause to bring claims against an agent of a contractual party so as to evade the jurisdiction clause. But this was probably not the right reading of *The Hornbay*.

(d) Further, in *Winnetka Trading Corpn v Julius Baer* [2009] Bus LR 1006, §§28–29 (not an anti-suit case), Lord Scott's comments in *Donohue* at §61 were followed to support a finding that litigating against a connected third party may well be a breach of an exclusive jurisdiction clause.

FN 54. For a recent example of consideration of whether a jurisdiction clause should be read as exclusive or non-exclusive, see *Bank of New York Mellon v GV Films* [2010] 1 Lloyd's Rep 365, §§10–15. **7.21**

FN 56. See also *Sea Trade Maritime Corp v Hellenic Mutual War Risks Association (Bermuda) Ltd (The Athena)* [2006] 2 CLC 710, following *Pathe Screen Entertainment Ltd v Handmade Films (Distributors) Ltd* (Hobhouse J, 11 July 1989).

7.22 FN 62. The principles outlined in *Fiona Trust* apply to jurisdiction clauses as much as to arbitration clauses: *Skype Technologies SA v Joltid* [2009] EWHC 2783 (Ch), §§14–19.

FN 63. A number of recent decisions have provided further guidance as to the categories of foreign proceedings which will be treated as not being in breach of an exclusive jurisdiction clause.

(a) In *Midgulf International Ltd v Groupe Chimiche Tunisien* [2009] 2 Lloyds Rep 411, §59, Teare J had held that an action before the Tunisian courts for a declaration as to the validity of an English arbitration clause was not a breach of the clause, nor a breach of any implied agreement that the English court as the court of the seat would be the sole court to exercise supervisory jurisdiction. But the Court of Appeal disagreed, holding that proceedings abroad to declare invalid a valid English forum clause would be a 'repudiatory' breach of that clause: [2010] EWCA Civ 66, §52. *Sed quaere*?

(b) There are now a number of authorities illustrating the proposition that either the commencement of, or resistance to, enforcement proceedings abroad will not usually be a breach of an exclusive jurisdiction clause which requires proceedings on the merits to be determined in England: *Shashoua v Sharma* [2009] 2 Lloyds Rep 376, §§40–41; *Vitol SA v Capri Marine Ltd (No 2)* [2010] EWHC 458 (Comm), §§29–35. See also *Masri v Consolidated Contractors International Co SAL (No 3)* [2009] QB 503, where no attempt was made to restrain proceedings brought abroad to resist enforcement of an English judgment. In contrast, however, attempts to use the foreign proceedings to challenge the validity of the English award or judgment, or to relitigate the matter under dispute, were restrained in *Shashoua v Sharma* and *Masri (No 3)* respectively.

(c) In *Bank of New York Mellon v GV Films* [2010] 1 Lloyd's Rep 365, §20, Field J observed in passing that it would have been inappropriate to restrain by injunction Indian corporate law proceedings relating to the demerger of an Indian company which was a debtor under a contract containing an English jurisdiction clause.

7.23 FN 64. See further the comments under §7.18 of this Supplement.

7.24 FN 66. See also *Elektrim SA v Vivendi Holdings 1 Corporation* [2009] 1 Lloyds Rep 59 (CA).

For recent discussion of severability, see *Deutsche Bank v Asia Pacific Broadband Wireless Communications Inc* [2008] 2 Lloyds Rep 619 (CA). **7.27**

F. INJUNCTIONS IN SUPPORT OF A FOREIGN FORUM

FN 90. In *Sheffield United FC Ltd v West Ham United FC Plc* [2009] 1 Lloyds Rep 167, §40, Teare J accepted in passing that an anti-suit injunction to enforce an arbitration clause fell within the court's supervisory jurisdiction. **7.33**

G. INJUNCTIONS TO ENFORCE ARBITRATION CLAUSES

FN 93. In *AES UST-Kamenogorsk Hydropower Plant LLP v UST-Kamenogorsk Hydropower Plant JSC* [2010] EWHC 772 (Comm), it was held that section 37(1) of the Senior Courts Act 1981 (and not section 44 of the Arbitration Act 1996) was the appropriate provision for the grant of anti-suit injunctions to enforce an arbitration clause. The argument that it could not be engaged if no arbitration had been commenced or was likely to be commenced was rejected: §§19–20. **7.36**

FN 94. Consistently with the proposition in the main text, in *Steamship Mutual Underwriting Association (Bermuda) Ltd v Sulpicio Lines Inc* [2008] 2 Lloyds Rep 269, §28, Walker J held that there was nothing in section 1 of the 1996 Act which precluded the grant of an anti-suit injunction to enforce an arbitration clause. However, the learned judge relied on the reasoning of *Vale do Rio Doce Navegacao SA v Shanghai Bao Steel Ocean Shipping Co Ltd* [2000] 2 Lloyds Rep 1, which does not clearly support the proposition.

In *AES UST-Kamenogorsk Hydropower Plant LLP v UST-Kamenogorsk Hydropower Plant JSC* [2010] EWHC 772 (Comm), it was argued that an injunction to enforce an arbitration clause would be precluded by section 1(c) if no arbitration had been commenced nor was likely to be. This proposition was rejected: §§18–21. Arguments to the contrary based on *Vale do Rio* were rejected.

FN 95. In *Sheffield United FC Ltd v West Ham United FC Plc* [2009] 1 Lloyds Rep 167, §§37–41, the parties were agreed that they had agreed to arbitrate before a Football Association arbitration tribunal but disagreed over **7.37** whether an appeal lay from that tribunal to the Court of Arbitration for Sport in Lausanne, Switzerland ('CAS'), a private arbitration institution. West Ham appealed to the CAS and Sheffield United applied for an anti-suit injunction from the English courts to restrain them from doing so. In this situation, it was tactically possible for West Ham to make an application under section 9 of the Arbitration Act 1996, and they did so, although the application failed, as Teare J held that section 9 was not engaged (for the reasons discussed under §7.38 in this Supplement below).

7.38 In *Sheffield United FC Ltd v West Ham United FC Plc* [2009] 1 Lloyds Rep 167, §§37–41, an application was made under section 9 of the Arbitration Act 1996 to stay a claim for an anti-suit injunction to enforce an arbitration agreement. Teare J concluded that the stay application should be refused, because (i) the power to grant an anti-suit injunction to enforce an arbitration clause was part of the court's supervisory jurisdiction over arbitrations; (ii) the class of disputes covered by the arbitration clause (which was in standard form, covering disputes 'arising out of or in connection with' the contract) did not encompass 'a dispute as to whether the court should exercise its supervisory jurisdiction'; and (iii) 'whilst the parties have agreed to arbitration they have also agreed, by reason of the seat of the arbitration being England, that the English court is the appropriate court to exercise a supervisory jurisdiction in support of the arbitration' (relying on *C v D* [2008] 1 Lloyds Rep 239 (CA), §17).

Teare J went on to observe that his analysis was the 'same as or similar to that suggested' in §7.38 of the original text of this work (at §40 of his judgment). That is so, but it is submitted that the learned judge's answer at (ii) above is more elegant. On the other hand, the proposition at (iii), although established by authority of the Court of Appeal in *C v D*, is disputable. The better analysis is possibly that the parties' implied agreement arising out of the arbitration clause is that supervisory proceedings *may* be brought in England to protect an English arbitration, rather than an agreement that supervisory proceedings *may not* be brought anywhere else: see Ch 7, §§7.38, 7.42 of the main text of this work.

7.39 In *Steamship Mutual Underwriting Association (Bermuda) Ltd v Sulpicio Lines Inc* [2008] 2 Lloyds Rep 269, §33, Walker J observed *obiter* (at an uncontested hearing) that an arbitrator could grant an anti-suit injunction.

In support of the proposition that arbitrators can grant anti-suit awards under section 48(5) of the 1996 Act see S Dutson, M Howarth, 'After West Tankers—rise of the "foreign torpedo"' (2009) 75 Arbitration 334, 345.

However, Professor Charles Debattista has suggested (relying on *Kastner v Jason* [2005] 1 Lloyds Rep 397 (CA), §16) that, as the arbitrators' powers under section 48(5) of the 1996 Act are confined to 'substantive awards', the powers thereby conferred cannot extend to anti-suit injunctions: see C Debattista, 'Arbitrators' powers to order interim measures including anti-suit injunctions' (2010) 76 Arbitration 421, 425. It is respectfully submitted that this does not follow. *Kastner v Jason* held only that section 48(5) was confined to 'final awards and substantive remedies on the merits'—which did not include a freezing injunction. This does indeed preclude an *interim* anti-suit award being made by arbitrators. But there is no doubt that (as discussed in Ch 3 of this work) anti-suit injunctions can be granted by the court by way of final relief. In the circumstances, there is no reason why they should not be awarded by way of final award by arbitrators under the powers conferred by section 48(5).

The decision in *C v D* [2008] 1 Lloyds Rep 239 (CA) was followed in *Sheffield United FC Ltd v West Ham United FC Plc* [2009] 1 Lloyds Rep 167, §40; and *Shashoua v Sharma* [2009] 2 Lloyds Rep 376. For a further example of the force of the English court's assumption that it alone is qualified to hear challenges to English arbitration awards, see *Sheltam Rail Co (Pty) Ltd v Mirambo Holdings* [2008] 2 Lloyds Rep 195, §37 (arguably, an illegitimate interference with the foreign courts' jurisdiction over enforcement: see §5.54 of this Supplement). In *Midgulf International Ltd v Groupe Chimiche Tunisien* [2009] 2 Lloyd's Rep 411, §52, the Court of Appeal, without express reference to *C v D*, took an analogous approach, concluding that an application to a foreign court to declare that an actually valid English arbitration clause was not binding would be a repudiation of the arbitration clause; or alternatively could be restrained in the interests of justice if it amounted to an attempt to derail a valid English arbitration. **7.42**

H. FOREIGN PROCEEDINGS TO OBTAIN SECURITY

As Jonathan Hirst QC observed in *Kallang Shipping SA Panama v Axa Assurances Senegal (The Kallang) (No 2)* [2009] 1 Lloyds Rep 124, §78: **7.43**

> the English court will not restrain a party to an English arbitration clause from arresting a vessel in another jurisdiction where the sole purpose of the arrest is to obtain reasonable security for the claim to be arbitrated or litigated in England. Section 11 of the Arbitration Act 1996 also assumes that a claimant can properly arrest a vessel in order to obtain security for an arbitration claim. The precise basis on which the court acts—construction of the arbitration clause or discretion—is not authoritatively established but the general approach is clear enough. Where, however, the claimants' actions go beyond simply seeking reasonable security for the arbitration proceedings, there is a breach of the arbitration clause which the English court may restrain.

7.44 FN 117: Another ground of distinction from *Mantovani v Carapelli*, in respect of arbitrations governed by the Arbitration Act 1996 (like almost all arbitrations current today), is that that case was decided before the passing of sections 26 of the Civil Jurisdiction and Judgments Act 1982, and section 11 of the Arbitration Act 1996, both of which recognize the legitimacy of applications for security to English courts in support of arbitration proceedings or exclusive jurisdiction clauses. It is arguable that these provisions indirectly support the contention that modern arbitration or exclusive jurisdiction clauses should not be read to prohibit reasonable applications for security being made in foreign courts.

FNs 118 and 119: see also *Kallang Shipping SA Panama v Axa Assurances Senegal (The Kallang) (No 2)* [2009] 1 Llyods Rep 124, §§78–79; *Sotrade Denizcilik Sanayi Ve Ticaret AS v Amadou Lo (The Duden)* [2009] 1 Lloyds Rep 145, §§55–62; and *Green Flower Navigation Malta Ltd v SC Santierul Naval SA Constanta* (Unreported, 7 June 2002), §20–23.

Brave Bulk Transport Ltd v Spot on Shipping Ltd [2009] 2 Lloyds Rep 115 concerned proceedings in New York against X, in which an attempt was made to enforce an English default judgment which had in fact been granted against Y, by means of an 'alter ego' doctrine available under US law. It was held that the New York proceedings were not, on the facts of the case, a breach of an exclusive jurisdiction clause in the original contract to which X had been party with the claimant. This was followed in *Vitol SA v Capri Marine Ltd (No 2)* [2010] EWHC 458 (Comm), §§29–34.

FN 120. In *Kallang Shipping SA Panama v Axa Assurances Senegal (The Kallang) (No 2)* [2009] 1 Lloyds Rep 124, §§65–86, Jonathan Hirst QC rejected the analysis that seeking to compel the other party to abandon its contractual rights to arbitrate was a breach of implied terms of the arbitration agreement, but reached the same conclusion as a matter of express terms:

> If one party tried to obtain security for proceedings in another jurisdiction or to force the other party to give up his right to arbitrate disputes, this would be a direct and straightforward breach of the arbitration clause. (§79)

See also *Sotrade Denizcilik Sanayi Ve Ticaret AS v Amadou Lo (The Duden)* [2009] 1 Lloyds Rep 145, §§55–62.

FN 122. It may be that the correct analysis is that if adequate alternative security is offered in England, then security proceedings abroad are no longer 'reasonable' and are therefore a breach of contract: *Kallang Shipping SA Panama v Axa Assurances Senegal (The Kallang) (No 2)* [2009] 1 Lloyds Rep 124, §78.

FN 125. See *Kallang Shipping SA Panama v Axa Assurances Senegal (The Kallang) (No 2)* [2009] 1 Lloyds Rep 124, where the analysis adopted was that only applications abroad seeking 'reasonable' security were consistent with the arbitration clause. If this is the right analysis, then it will follow that, in respect of other categories of interim applications abroad (such as applications for the deposition of witnesses), there will presumably be a distinction between, on the one hand, 'reasonable' applications abroad which legitimately support the arbitration, and on the other hand, applications abroad which cut across the arbitration clause and will therefore be a breach of contract.

8

Strong Reasons and Discretion

B. THE NATURE OF THE CLAUSE

In *Ace Capital Ltd v CMS Energy Corp* [2008] 2 CLC 318, the contract combined an English arbitration clause and a US service of suit clause. Christopher Clarke J concluded that as a matter of construction the US service of suit clause did not qualify the arbitration clause, and therefore that US proceedings on the merits were a breach of the arbitration agreement. On that basis, he held that the presence of the service of suit clause was not good reason to refuse to grant the injunction. **8.04**

C. THE NATURE OF THE LITIGATION

The views expressed in this paragraph were approved in *Morgan Stanley & Co International Plc v China Haisheng Juice Holdings Co Ltd* [2010] 1 Lloyd's Rep 265, §37 and *Skype Technologies SA v Joltid* [2009] EWHC 2783 (Ch), §33. **8.06**

In *Bank of New York Mellon v GV Films* [2010] 1 Lloyd's Rep 365, the exclusive jurisdiction clause expressly waived either party's right to contend that the chosen court was an inconvenient forum. Field J held that this was a matter of great weight, so that especially strong grounds would be required before the exclusive jurisdiction clause could be departed from on grounds founded on convenience, or before it could be held that there were 'strong reasons' not to enforce the clause by injunction.

See also *Deutsche Bank AG v Sebastian Holdings Inc* [2009] 2 CLC 949, §§18–24; *Vitol SA v Arcturus Merchant Trust* [2009] Bus LR 271, §§29–30.

8.07 The views expressed in this paragraph of the original text were approved in *Morgan Stanley & Co International Plc v China Haisheng Juice Holdings Co Ltd* [2010] 1 Lloyds Rep 265, §37.

However, in *Deutsche Bank AG v Sebastian Holdings Inc* [2009] 2 CLC 949, §24, Burton J suggested that potential problems with overlapping proceedings might well be foreseeable, 'if, as here, the parties entered into a series of interlinked agreements with different jurisdiction clauses'.

8.08 FN 14. However, cf *contra Deutsche Bank AG v Sebastian Holdings Inc* [2009] 2 CLC 949, §24.

FN 16. See also *Skype Technologies SA v Joltid* [2009] EWHC 2783 (Ch), §§34–35; *Morgan Stanley & Co International Plc v China Haisheng Juice Holdings Co Ltd* [2010] 1 Lloyds Rep 265.

D. THE CONDUCT OF THE INJUNCTION CLAIMANT

8.11 FN 22. See also *Shashoua v Sharma* [2009] 2 Lloyds Rep 376, §44.

FNs 23 and 29. See also *Transfield Shipping Inc v Chiping Xinfa Huayu Alumina Co Ltd* [2009] EWHC 3629 (QB), §§71–79.

8.12 FN 33. Participation in foreign proceedings under protest and under a reserve as to jurisdiction will not usually be treated as a strong reason not to grant the injunction: see *Bank of New York Mellon v GV Films* [2010] 1 Lloyd's Rep 365, §§19, 22. Similarly, in *Shashoua v Sharma* [2009] 2 Lloyds Rep 376, §§46–48 (where a mini-trial of the question of voluntary submission was ordered), it was observed that if the injunction claimant had submitted to the jurisdiction of the foreign court as a technical matter of foreign law, that would be a much less forceful point against the grant of the injunction than an unequivocal and deliberate voluntary submission to the jurisdiction of the foreign court.

E. COMITY

8.19–8.20 In *Rimpacific Navigation Inc v Daehan Shipbuilding Co Ltd (The Jin Man)* [2009] EWHC 2941, the background facts were that a director of a Korean company had signed guarantees purportedly on its behalf containing English law and English exclusive jurisdiction clauses. The Korean company argued that it was not bound by his signature, and relied on Korean law to suggest he had neither actual or ostensible authority. Parallel proceedings were brought in England and Korea. David Steel J granted an anti-suit injunction. Applying the conventional English conflict of laws rule, he held that the ostensible authority of the director was determined by English law as the law of the putative contract, and that applying English law, there was a strongly arguable case on the facts that the director did have ostensible authority to sign the guarantees. He was also of the view that the same result would probably follow as a matter of Korean law, but the position was less clear.

In considering questions of good reason and discretion, David Steel J observed that the claimants had a justified concern that, if the proceedings in Korea continued, there was a real risk that in the Korean courts the authority of Mr Oh might be considered without regard to English law (apparently because Korean conflict rules would apply the law of the company's place of incorporation to questions of authority), and that this might lead to an adverse *res judicata* issue estoppel. This was regarded as a ground in favour of the grant of the injunction. This is a striking example of the English court's willingness to assume that it is right to impose its own conflict of laws rules on other legal systems, without needing to identify any system-transcendent justification.

For a further example of the robust approach taken by English courts to the conflict of conflicts, see *Vitol SA v Arcturus Merchant Trust* [2009] Bus LR 271, §§33–34 (following *OT Africa Line Ltd v Magic Sportswear Corpn* [2005] 2 Lloyds Rep 170).

9

Non-Exclusive Jurisdiction Clauses

B. IMPLIED TERMS

FN 6. A slightly different analysis of Waller LJ's decision in *Sabah*, viewing it as based on a finding of a contractual obligation, was adopted in *Deutsche Bank AG v Highland Crusader Offshore Partners* [2010] 1 WLR 1023 (CA), §112. **9.04**

FN 7. The decision in *Sabah* has since been restrictively distinguished by the Court of Appeal in *Deutsche Bank AG v Highland Crusader Offshore Partners* [2010] 1 WLR 1023 (CA).

FN 9. These doubts have been in part dispelled, and the law put back on the right track, by the Court of Appeal's decision in *Deutsche Bank AG v Highland Crusader Offshore Partners* [2010] 1 WLR 1023 (CA), where *Sabah* was restrictively distinguished, and Toulson LJ observed that: **9.05**

> In terms of contract law, I cannot see how a party could ordinarily be said to be in breach of a contract containing a non-exclusive jurisdiction clause merely by pursuing proceedings in an alternative jurisdiction. (at §105)

The result of *Deutsche v Highland* is that it will only be in cases of specific and unusual wording which demand a different approach that a non-exclusive jurisdiction clause will be held to include an implied term prohibiting parallel litigation abroad.

Following *Deutsche Bank AG v Highland Crusader Offshore Partners* [2010] 1 WLR 1023 (CA), §105, it will only be in cases of unusual wording that a non-exclusive jurisdiction clause will be held to include an implied term prohibiting parallel litigation abroad. So, in respect of the third situation discussed, a term will not usually be implied to prohibit duplicative proceedings in a foreign forum even if those are commenced later than proceedings in the selected forum. **9.06**

C. INDIRECT RELEVANCE WHERE THERE IS NO IMPLIED TERM

9.07–9.11 Paragraphs 9.07–9.11 of the main text of this work were referred to with approval by Carnwath LJ in *Deutsche Bank AG v Highland Crusader Offshore Partners* [2010] 1 WLR 1023 (CA), §126. This case has received favourable comment in CJS Knight, 'Anti-suit injunctions and non-exclusive jurisdiction clauses' [2010] 69(1) CLJ 25.

9.08 FN 15. See also *Deutsche Bank AG v Highland Crusader Offshore Partners* [2010] 1 WLR 1023 (CA), §64.

9.09 In *Deutsche Bank AG v Highland Crusader Offshore Partners* [2010] 1 WLR 1023 (CA), §§64, 105–110, Toulson LJ considered that the very nature of a non-exclusive jurisdiction clause 'leaves open' the possibility that there may be another appropriate jurisdiction (at §64). His reasoning probably negates the proposition that, in most cases, the presence of a non-exclusive jurisdiction clause will significantly lighten the burden of proving vexation and oppression (at §§105–110). The heart of Toulson LJ's analysis is that non-exclusive forum clauses should only give any sort of priority or dominance to the selected forum where they have specific wording that supports this (at §108), and that in general it is wrong to conclude that the presence of a non-exclusive forum clause creates a presumption that parallel proceedings are vexatious and oppressive (at §§106–107). In reaching his conclusions, he referred with approval to §9.12 of the main text of this work.

9.10 The reasoning in §9.10 of the main text of this work, and the restrictive distinction of *Sabah* there proposed, was largely adopted by the Court of Appeal in *Deutsche Bank AG v Highland Crusader Offshore Partners* [2010] 1 WLR 1023 (CA), §§85, 112.

9.11 In *Deutsche Bank AG v Highland Crusader Offshore Partners* [2010] 1 WLR 1023 (CA), §§85, 105–114, it was held that any such rigid approach derived from *Sabah* was not the law.

9.12 This paragraph was adopted by Toulson LJ in the Court of Appeal's decision in *Deutsche Bank AG v Highland Crusader Offshore Partners* [2010] 1 WLR 1023 (CA), §105.

10

Quasi-Contractual Anti-Suit Injunctions

B. DERIVED RIGHTS AND FORUM CLAUSES

FN 7. See also *Whitesea Shipping and Trading Corporation v El Paso Rio Clara Ltda* [2010] 1 Lloyds Rep 648, §21. **10.06**

D. THIRD PARTY RIGHTS UNDER FOREIGN LAW

See also *Vitol SA v Arcturus Merchant Trust* [2009] Bus LR 271, §36. **10.13**

11

Injunctions to Restrain Arbitration Proceedings

A. INJUNCTIONS TO RESTRAIN ARBITRATIONS IN ENGLAND

FN 4. The approach in *Workplace Technologies v E Squared Ltd*, suggesting that a void adjudication could not be restrained by injunction, was not followed in Scotland: *Naylor v Greenacres Curling Ltd* [2001] SLT 1092, §§9–10. **11.02**

FN 23. Further authority has subsequently confirmed that injunctions can be granted at common law to restrain adjudications under the Housing, Grants, Construction and Regeneration Act 1996. Adjudications are not covered by the Arbitration Act 1996 and the Housing, Grants, Construction and Regeneration Act 1996 does not preclude the grant of the injunction. However, such injunctions should only be granted rarely: *Dorchester Hotel v Vivid Interiors Ltd* [2009] Bus LR 1026, §§15, 17. See *contra Mentmore Towers Ltd v Packman Lucas Ltd* [2010] BLR 393, where standard principles of vexation and oppression were applied; but it was apparently not argued that any higher threshold should be surpassed. **11.06**

In *China Petroleum and Development Corporation v LG Caltex Gas Co Ltd* (Unreported, 5 December 2000), pp 10–16, Andrew Smith J held that section 1(c) of the Arbitration Act 1996 did not remove the court's common law power to restrain the pursuit of an arbitration over which the tribunal has no jurisdiction, even where the injunction claimant had taken part in the arbitration and so could not rely on section 72 of the 1996 Act. However, the injunction was declined in the court's discretion because it had been sought too late. **11.09–11.10**

11.13 FNs 35–37. The distinctions drawn in the original text were treated as the law in *Broda Agro Trade (Cyprus) Limited v Alfred C Toepfer International Gmbh* [2010] 1 Lloyds Rep 353, §29. In that case, a party who had made extensive submissions on the merits to the Tribunal was held to have 'taken part' in the arbitration: see §§30–36.

B. INJUNCTIONS TO RESTRAIN ARBITRATIONS OUTSIDE THE JURISDICTION

11.18 See eg *Sheffield United FC Ltd v West Ham United FC Plc* [2009] 1 Lloyds Rep 167.

11.20 FNs 51 and 52. In *Sheffield United FC Ltd v West Ham United FC Plc* [2009] 1 Lloyds Rep 167, §§26–27, it was common ground that the parties had agreed to arbitrate before a Football Association arbitration tribunal in England. However, West Ham sought to appeal from the arbitration award to the Court of Arbitration for Sport in Lausanne, Switzerland ('CAS'). Sheffield United sought an anti-suit injunction restraining West Ham's pursuit of the CAS proceedings, contending that the parties had agreed that the decision of the arbitration tribunal was final, and that they had not agreed that appeal should lie to the CAS. West Ham's arguments included the contention that the CAS should determine its own jurisdiction. Teare J held, it is submitted correctly, that *Weissfisch v Julius* [2006] 1 Lloyds Rep 716 (CA) could be distinguished, and it was appropriate to grant an injunction. Whereas *Weissfisch* concerned an arbitration whose seat was abroad, and the validity of an arbitration clause that would be governed by foreign law, this case concerned a potential appeal against an arbitration award given in an arbitration with an English seat and subject to an English law arbitration clause. Further, Teare J had already concluded that, on a true construction of the relevant arbitration rules, which were governed by English law, the argument that the parties had agreed that an appeal might lie to the CAS had no real prospects of success. So 'it is not at all clear why it is appropriate for CAS to determine an argument which has not been and probably cannot be articulated' (§28(i)). Consequently, on the unusual facts of this case, it was appropriate to seek a remedy from the court of the seat of the original arbitration rather than the purported foreign appeal tribunal.

11.21 See also now *Sheffield United FC Ltd v West Ham United FC Plc* [2009] 1 Lloyds Rep 167.

11.22 FN 58. This proposition is also exemplified by *Sheffield United FC Ltd v West Ham United FC Plc* [2009] 1 Lloyds Rep 167.

C. INJUNCTIONS AGAINST ARBITRATORS

FN 64. In *Mentmore Towers Ltd v Packman Lucas Ltd* [2010] BLR 393, injunctions were granted to restrain adjudications under the Housing Grants, Construction and Regeneration Act 1996, but they were directed against the party initiating the adjudications and not the adjudicator. **11.23**

FN 66. See further *Jivraj v Hashwani* [2010] EWCA Civ 72, §§14, 21–23.

It may be that the English courts' recent trend of concluding that the courts of the seat of the arbitration are entitled to absolute deference is waning: see *Dallah Real Estate & Tourism Holding Co v Pakistan* [2010] 2 WLR 805 (CA), §§59, 90–91. **11.24**

12

Anti-Suit Injunctions and European Jurisdictional Law

A. INTRODUCTION

FN 1. The New Lugano Convention has been ratified by the EU and Norway, and is now in force as between the EU and Norway with effect from 1 January 2010: see Civil Jurisdiction and Judgments Regulations 2009, SI 2009/3131. Pursuant to a decision of the Swiss Federal Council of 31 March 2010, Switzerland will ratify the Convention with effect from 1 January 2011. It has not yet been ratified by Iceland. **12.01**

It appears from C-195/07, *Allianz AG v West Tankers Inc (The Front Comor)* [2009] ECR I-663, that the principles outlined in *Turner v Grovit* apply only if the court of the other member state, before which proceedings are sought to be restrained, would otherwise be exercising or considering whether to exercise a Brussels–Lugano jurisdiction: see at §§24–25, 28. The principle of mutual trust does not apply to prevent injunctions being granted in respect of proceedings before the courts of other Brussels–Lugano states which are outside the material scope of the Brussels–Lugano regime. **12.04**

12.04 FN 10. However, in the case of *In Zone Brands International Inc v In Beverage International*, Cass 1re civ, 14 October 2009, No 08-16.369 and No 08-16.549, the French Cour de Cassation upheld a decision to enforce in France an American anti-suit injunction to enforce a jurisdiction clause in favour of the courts of the state of Georgia. Arguments that the anti-suit injunction wrongfully interfered with the sovereignty of the French judge or was contrary to public international law were rejected. However, the approval of the Cour de Cassation was limited to the situtation where an anti-suit injunction was sought to enforce a jurisdiction clause, outside the scope of EC law. The Cour de Cassation has therefore apparently moved away from the earlier critical attitude manifested in *Stolzenberg v Daimler Chrysler Canada Inc* [2005] ILPr 24. See the discussion of *In Zone Brands* in JDI 2010, p 146, Note S Clavel.

FN 11. The European Court of Justice's disquieting habit of deciding to abolish common law institutions in the absence of the judges whose legal systems are most closely concerned was continued in C-195/07, *Allianz AG v West Tankers Inc (The Front Comor)* [2009] ECR I-663, where the Irish judge, but not the English judge, was part of the panel. (It can also be noted that the advocate general in *Turner v Grovit*, where the injunction sought restrained proceedings before the Courts of Spain, was Spanish. In the *Front Comor*, on the other hand, where the proceedings restrained were Italian, the advocate general was German.)

12.05 The continuity of interpretation of the Brussels–Lugano regime has been repeatedly re-affirmed: see eg: C-533/07, *Falco Privatstiftung v Weller-Lindhorst* [2010] Bus LR 210, ECJ §§52, 53, 56.

12.06 The conclusion, that the restrictions imposed on anti-suit injunctions by the Brussels–Lugano regime are restrictions of *power* and not merely *jurisdiction*, has been reinforced in C-195/07, *Allianz AG v West Tankers Inc (The Front Comor)* [2009] ECR I-663, where the European Court of Justice accepted that anti-suit injunctions to enforce an arbitration clause were outside the scope of the Brussels–Lugano regime for jurisdictional purposes (§§22–23), but were nevertheless prohibited from being granted by the principle of *effet utile* under European law, because they interfered with the proper operation of the Brussels–Lugano regime (§§24–32).

12.07 In C-195/07, *Allianz AG v West Tankers Inc (The Front Comor)* [2009] ECR I-663, the European Court of Justice has now concluded that injunctions to enforce an arbitration clause are within the arbitration exception, and outside the Brussels–Lugano regime; but nevertheless are contrary to the principle of mutual trust and thus inconsistent with the Brussels–Lugano regime.

For academic discussion critical of the European Court of Justice's decision, see A Briggs, 'Fear and Loathing in Syracuse and Luxembourg' [2009]

LMCLQ 161; R Fentiman, 'Arbitration and Anti-Suit Injunctions in Europe' [2009] CLJ 278; S Dutson, M Howarth, 'After West Tankers—rise of the "foreign torpedo"' (2009) 75 Arbitration 334; J Tumbridge, 'European Anti-Suit Injunctions in favour of arbitration—a sea change?' [2010] ICCLR 177; H Seriki, 'Anti-Suit Injunctions, arbitration and the European Court of Justice' [2010] JBL 24; J Lurie, 'Court Intervention in arbitration: support or interference' (2010) 76 Arbitration 447, 449–450.

For academic discussion supportive of the European Court of Justice's approach, see K Lenaerts, 'The Contribution of the European Court of Justice to the area of freedom, security and justice' (2010) 59 ICLQ 255, 285–288. For a more nuanced approach, see JDI 2009, p 1281, Note B Audit.

B. BOTH SETS OF PROCEEDINGS WITHIN THE BRUSSELS–LUGANO REGIME AND ZONE

The analysis in these paragraphs is supported by C-195/07, *Allianz AG v West Tankers Inc (The Front Comor)* [2009] ECR I-663. **12.08–12.09**

C. COMPETING PROCEEDINGS OUTSIDE THE BRUSSELS–LUGANO ZONE

The reasoning in C-195/07, *Allianz AG v West Tankers Inc (The Front Comor)* **12.11**
[2009] ECR I-663 (leaving aside some elusive and glancing comments about the role of the New York Convention at §33, as to which see below), supports the proposition that the Brussels–Lugano regime imposes no substantive limitations on the grant of anti-suit injunctions to restrain the pursuit of proceedings outside the Brussels–Lugano zone. The European Court of Justice's reasoning for its conclusion that anti-suit injunctions to enforce arbitration clauses are inconsistent with the proper operation of the Brussels–Lugano regime was based (i) on the principle of mutual trust between member state courts; (ii) on the doctrine that the right of another member state court to assess whether or not it should exercise putative Brussels–Lugano jurisdiction could not be interfered with. Neither of these principles affects anti-suit injunctions to restrain proceedings before the courts of third countries.

The recent English authorities have all proceeded on the basis, and where necessary expressly found, that (i) the Brussels–Lugano regime does not affect the grant of anti-suit injunctions to restrain proceedings before the courts of third states; (ii) there is nothing in *The Front Comor* which could affect this conclusion; (iii) the English court's approach to granting anti-suit injunctions to restrain proceedings outside the Brussels–Lugano zone is unaffected by their prohibition within the Brussels–Lugano zone: see *Shashoua v Sharma* [2009] 2 Lloyds Rep 376, §§35–39; *Midgulf International Ltd v Groupe Chimiche Tunisien* [2009] 2 Lloyd's Rep 411, §§67–68.

For examples of cases where injunctions were granted to restrain the pursuit of non-European proceedings without any argument that this was impermissible even being advanced, see eg *Whitesea Shipping and Trading Corp v El Paso Rio Clara Ltda* [2010] 1 Lloyds Rep 647 (Brazil); *Morgan Stanley & Co International Plc v China Haisheng Juice Holdings Co Ltd* [2010] 1 Lloyds Rep 265 (China); *Bank of New York Mellon v GV Films* [2010] 1 Lloyd's Rep 365 (India); there are many other examples.

In its judgment in *The Front Comor*, the European Court of Justice had commented that the result it reached was supported by the New York Convention. This provided ammunition for a renewed attempt to raise the argument that the grant of anti-suit injunctions to enforce arbitration clauses is inconsistent with the New York Convention (which had previously been rejected by the English courts: see Ch 7 of the original text, §7.10 and FN 26). However, in *Shashoua v Sharma* [2009] 2 Lloyds Rep 376, §§35–39, Cooke J rejected this argument. He held that the European Court of Justice, and the advocate general, were concerned only to show that the conclusion they reached as to the inadmissibility of the anti-suit injunction within Europe was not inconsistent with the structure of the New York Convention. They were not concerned with and not deciding whether anti-suit injunctions were precluded by the New York Convention. The same conclusion was reached, in short terms, by the Court of Appeal in *Midgulf International Ltd v Groupe Chimiche Tunisien* [2010] EWCA Civ 66, §§67–68.

12.12 The decision of the Court of Appeal in *Masri v Consolidated Contractors (No 3)* [2009] QB 503, that the Brussels–Lugano regime had no jurisdictionally preclusive effect in respect of anti-suit injunctions, is unaffected by the reasoning in C-195/07, *Allianz AG v West Tankers Inc (The Front Comor)* [2009] ECR I-663.

D. INJUNCTIONS AND PROCEEDINGS IN THE UNITED KINGDOM

12.13–12.14 The conclusions reached in these paragraphs are unaffected by the decision in C-195/07, *Allianz AG v West Tankers Inc (The Front Comor)* [2009]

ECR I-663, with one exception: the poverty of the reasoning of the European Court of Justice in *The Front Comor* will make it all the more likely that the European Court of Justice's approach to the Brussels–Lugano regime will not be cross-applied within the UK by the English courts (see §12.14, text to FN 41).

These questions have now been answered 'Yes' and 'No' respectively by the European Court in C-195/07, *Allianz AG v West Tankers Inc (The Front Comor)* [2009] ECR I-663. **12.15**

The prediction in this paragraph has been confirmed by the European Court in C-195/07, *Allianz AG v West Tankers Inc (The Front Comor)* [2009] ECR I-663. **12.18**

For academic commentary on the European Court of Justice's decision, see §12.07 of this Supplement above.

In C-195/07, *Allianz AG v West Tankers Inc (The Front Comor)* [2009] ECR I-663, the European Court (correctly) viewed the arbitration exception question and the incompatibility question as analytically separate. It was therefore able to conclude that anti-suit injunctions to enforce arbitration clauses were 'arbitration' and thus excluded from the scope of the Brussels–Lugano regime, while still prohibiting anti-suit injunctions to enforce an arbitration clause by restraining the pursuit of proceedings within the Brussels–Lugano zone. **12.19–12.25**

The European Court's reasoning on the arbitration exception question derived from the application of both the 'subject matter' test and the 'rights which they serve to protect' test, which were applied indifferently and without apparent consideration of the potential inconsistency between the two tests (see §§22–23). However, in the case of an injunction to enforce an arbitration clause, both tests can be interpreted to produce much the same result, namely that such an injunction is 'arbitration'.

F. ANTI-SUIT INJUNCTIONS GRANTED BY ARBITRATORS

This question remains open following C-195/07, *Allianz AG v West Tankers Inc (The Front Comor)* [2009] ECR I-663. The European Court of Justice did not address this question and its reasoning does not necessitate either possible solution to the problem. **12.26**

FN 73. See *contra* the reasoning of C Debattista, 'Arbitrators' powers to order interim measures including anti-suit injunctions', Arbitration 2010, 76(3), 421, 425.

FN 75. The conclusion (i) that the principle of mutual trust does not apply to arbitrators was adopted by the arbitration tribunal in *CMA CGM v Hyundai MIPO Dockyard Co Ltd* [2009] 1 Lloyds Rep 213, §§35, 41–47, and although Burton J did not need to decide the point, he was sympathetic to the arbitrators' reasoning. The Tribunal reasoned in turn, and Burton J was minded to agree, that (ii) consequently arbitrators are not bound by the *res judicata* effect of Brussels–Lugano judgments which are to be recognized in England under the Brussels–Lugano regime. This latter conclusion (ii) was disapproved by the Court of Appeal in *National Navigation Co v Endesa Generacion SA (The Wadi Sudr)* [2010] 1 Lloyds Rep 193 (CA), §§56, 115–118. But the terms in which the Court of Appeal reached that decision did not involve reversing conclusion (i). Indeed, Moore-Bick LJ at §118 expressly accepted that 'it is quite true that the Regulation itself does not apply to arbitration tribunals.' The contention that arbitration tribunals are not affected by the principle of mutual trust thus probably reflects the English courts' understanding. Whether the European Court of Justice will agree remains to be seen.

12.27 In the light of the reasoning adopted by the European Court of Justice in C-195/07, *Allianz AG v West Tankers Inc (The Front Comor)* [2009] ECR I-663, it will not be possible to enforce an anti-suit award by entering court judgment in the terms of the award. The arbitrators may be outside the scope of the principle of mutual trust, but the court is not, and it is clear from the decision in *The Front Comor* that the mere fact that the English Court is itself operating outside the scope of the Brussels–Lugano regime does not immunize it from needing to respect the principle of mutual trust. See *National Navigation Co v Endesa Generacion SA (The Wadi Sudr)* [2010] 1 Lloyds Rep 193 (CA), §§56, 115–118, differing in this regard from *CMA CGM v Hyundai MIPO Dockyard Co Ltd* [2009] 1 Lloyds Rep 213, §§35, 41–47.

G. UNDERLYING PROCEEDINGS OUTSIDE THE MATERIAL SCOPE OF THE REGIME

12.29–12.33 As predicted in the original text, the European Court of Justice has decided *The Front Comor* by concluding that anti-suit injunctions to restrain the invocation of the Brussels–Lugano jurisdiction of another Brussels–Lugano court are inconsistent with the Brussels–Lugano regime, even if the proceedings they are sought to protect are outside the material scope of the regime: C-195/07, *Allianz AG v West Tankers Inc (The Front Comor)* [2009] ECR I-663. Lord Hoffmann's suggestions to the contrary are not the law.

Consequently, the issues explored in §§12.31–12.33 of the original text do not arise.

H. 'TARGET' PROCEEDINGS OUTSIDE THE SCOPE OF THE REGULATION

The European Court of Justice's reasoning in *The Front Comor* is tightly, and probably deliberately, focussed on the impermissibility of preventing the courts of another Brussels–Lugano member state from exercising their Brussels–Lugano jurisdiction, or from deciding for themselves whether they have Brussels–Lugano jurisdiction: C-195/07, *Allianz AG v West Tankers Inc (The Front Comor)* [2009] ECR I-663, §§24–30. It follows by inversion of this logic that the principle of mutual trust does not prevent anti-suit injunctions from restraining proceedings before other European courts which do not seek to invoke the Brussels–Lugano jurisdiction of those courts. **12.34**

In *Sheffield United FC Ltd v West Ham United FC Plc* [2009] 1 Lloyds Rep 167, §30, Teare J rejected an argument that the principle of mutual trust should preclude an anti-suit injunction to restrain proceedings before the Court of Arbitration for Sport, in Lausanne, Switzerland ('CAS'). He concluded that the principle of mutual trust only applied in respect of the courts of member states, and that CAS was a private body. **12.35**

K. DECLARATIONS

Text to FN 106. The conclusion that a claim for a declaration that an arbitration clause is binding is 'arbitration' and thus outside the scope of the Brussels–Lugano regime is now clearly correct, in the light of *Allianz AG v West Tankers Inc (The Front Comor)* [2009] ECR I-663, §§22–23. **12.39**

Text to FN 107. The European Court of Justice's reasoning in C-195/07, *Allianz AG v West Tankers Inc (The Front Comor)* [2009] ECR I-663 would suggest that declarations that an arbitration clause is binding are not inconsistent with the principle of mutual trust. The core of the European Court of Justice's reasoning was that it was impermissible to prevent a court of another member state from ruling on its own Brussels–Lugano jurisdiction (see §27). An anti-suit injunction, if complied with, would produce exactly this result. A declaration that an arbitration clause was binding might, or might not, have a *res judicata* effect in another state.

But it would not prevent the other state's court from ruling on its own Brussels–Lugano jurisdiction, since it could, for example, accept jurisdiction under the Brussels–Lugano regime and then stay proceedings in favour of arbitration under the New York Convention. Such a declaration could well be sought in a case where no specific proceedings in another Brussels–Lugano court were even contemplated.

The arguments about whether a declaration that an exclusive jurisdiction clause is binding is a legitimate remedy are more finely balanced; but it is submitted that the same result should follow as in the case of an arbitration clause. Provided that the declaration sought is framed as being about the effect and meaning of a contract, and no attempt is made to obtain a declaration directly as to whether the other Brussels–Lugano court has jurisdiction, there should be no infringement of the principle of mutual trust. Although the European Court of Justice noted, in *The Front Comor*, that it was exclusively for each Brussels–Lugano court to rule on its own jurisdiction (§28), a declaration that an exclusive jurisdiction clause is binding is not, strictly analysed, a ruling on the jurisdiction of the other court. Instead it is merely a conclusion on an issue which the other court may take into account if the declaration is recognized, under the recognition provisions of the Brussels–Lugano regime or otherwise. For academic commentary supporting this conclusion, see M-L Niboyet, 'Quelle sanction pour les accords sur la compétence après les arrêts *Turner* et *West Tankers*' 148–149 Gaz Pal (2009), pp 8–10. In *National Navigation Co v Endesa Generacion SA (The Wadi Sudr)* [2009] 1 Lloyds Rep 666, §§119–121, Gloster J rejected the submission that, in the light of *The Front Comor*, 'comity' should prevent her from making a declaration as to the incorporation of an arbitration clause, where proceedings were brought in another Brussels–Lugano court. Her judgment was overturned on appeal on other grounds, [2010] 1 Lloyds Rep 193 (CA), in terms which cast no doubt on the court's ability in principle to grant such declarations. However, see *contra* the doubts of CJS Knight, 'Arbitration and Litigation after *West Tankers*' [2009] LMCLQ 285, 289.

L. CLAIMS FOR DAMAGES

12.40 It remains unclear whether claims for damages for breach of exclusive jurisdiction agreements are inconsistent with the principle of mutual trust. The reasoning of the European Court of Justice in C-195/07, *Allianz AG v West Tankers Inc (The Front Comor)* [2009] ECR I-663 took a different path in certain respects to its earlier reasoning in C-159/02, *Turner v Grovit*

[2004] ECR I-3565. In particular, there was no focus on the anti-suit injunction being a 'penalty', nor any express reference to the illegitimacy of 'assessing' the jurisdiction of another Brussels–Lugano court. The European Court's reasoning in *The Front Comor* was more formalistic than it had been in *Turner v Grovit*. It included two main elements. The principal strand of reasoning was that injunctions which prevented another member state's court from assessing its own Brussels–Lugano jurisdiction were impermissible (§28). Damages do not have any preventative effect. But the European Court had also observed earlier in the judgment that it was exclusively for each Brussels–Lugano court to rule on its own jurisdiction (§27). The weight and exact interpretation to be put on this earlier element is not entirely clear, but there might be an argument that claims for damages illegitimately seek to rule, at least implicitly, on the legitimacy of the other court's exercise or potential exercise of Brussels–Lugano jurisdiction (see M-L Niboyet, 'Quelle sanction pour les accords sur la compétence après les arrêts *Turner* et *West Tankers*' 148–149 Gaz Pal (2009), pp 8–10).

The European Court of Justice's answer will, however, be driven not by formal application of the reasoning in its existing judgment but rather by assessment of the competing policy considerations. The danger that damages claims could lead to conflict between Brussels–Lugano courts could militate against acceptance of their legitimacy. But, on the other hand, the European court's lack of willingness to support contractual exclusive forum clauses has been strongly criticized by legal scholars across Europe, while in the context of the current review of the Brussels I Regulation, the other European institutions have also supported a range of proposals tending to give greater support to the enforcement of such clauses. Claims for damages are also well known in other member states and therefore do not suffer from the 'Not invented here' syndrome which has plagued the anti-suit injunction (although it is worth noting that in many other national laws, exclusive forum clauses are viewed as procedural obligations which do not create the full scope of contractual rights and duties). It is therefore possible that the gradual turning of the tide in the European debate could increase the chances that the damages claims will be distinguished from anti-suit injunctions.

For academic commentary suggesting that the damages remedy is not precluded by the principle of mutual trust, see A Briggs, *Agreements on Jurisdiction and Choice of Law* (2008), §§8.63–8.75. For the opposite point of view, see J Harris, 'Agreements on jurisdiction and choice of law: where next?' [2009] LMCLQ 537, 546–547.

In *CMA CGM v Hyundai MIPO Dockyard Co Ltd* [2009] 1 Lloyds Rep 213, damages were awarded by the Tribunal in respect of the result of proceedings in **12.41**

France brought in breach of an arbitration clause. It appears to have been assumed that this was legitimate in principle and no point was taken on the application of the principle of mutual trust.

Text to FN 116. This point does not arise, now that the European Court of Justice has disagreed with Lord Hoffmann's approach, in C-195/07, *Allianz AG v West Tankers Inc (The Front Comor)* [2009] ECR I-663.

Text to FN 117. The reasoning here gains some support from the European Court of Justice's decision in C-195/07, *Allianz AG v West Tankers Inc (The Front Comor)* [2009] ECR I-663. See §12.40 of this Supplement.

13

Interim Anti-Suit Injunctions

B. POWER AND NATURE

FN 7. *Fourie v Le Roux* was referred to by Lord Collins of Mapesbury in *Secretary of State for the Environment, Food and Rural Affairs v Meier* [2009] 1 WLR 2780, §97. **13.04**

Section 44 of the Arbitration Act 1996 refers to an application being made to the court by a party, or proposed party, to the arbitral proceedings. Consequently, it can only support interim relief where there is an existing or intended arbitration, and cannot support interim relief where neither the applicant nor the respondent intends to arbitrate (for example where the respondent wishes to litigate outside arbitration, while the applicant wishes not to litigate at all, but wishes to ensure that any litigation the respondent intends to bring will be arbitrated). See *AES UST-Kamenogorsk Hydropower Plant LLP v UST-Kamenogorsk Hydropower Plant JSC* [2010] EHC 772, §§18(i), 19(i), 20. However, interim injunctions in such a situation can in contrast be granted under section 37 of the Senior Courts Act 1981: see *AES UST* at §§18(ii)–(iii), 20–24. **13.08**

FN 13. Artificial or not, the 'asset' analysis was adopted in *Sheffield United FC Ltd v West Ham United FC Plc* [2009] 1 Lloyds Rep 167, §31.

After text to FN 14. A third barrier under section 44, if it applies, is the requirement in Arbitration Act 1996, s 44(5) that 'the arbitral tribunal has no power or is unable for the time being to act effectively'. This was held to be satisfied on the special facts of the case in *Sheffield United FC Ltd v West Ham United FC Plc* [2009] 1 Lloyds Rep 167. It is submitted that it will generally be satisfied, since arbitral tribunals cannot grant interim injunctions (see Ch 13, §13.11), and also because of their inability to grant remedies for contempt of court, which renders any anti-suit award relatively toothless (see Ch 7, §7.40).

FN 16. See also *Sheffield United FC Ltd v West Ham United FC Plc* [2009] 1 Lloyds Rep 167, §33.

FN 18. In *Sheffield United FC Ltd v West Ham United FC Plc* [2009] 1 Lloyds Rep 167, §31, Teare J accepted that an interim anti-suit injunction to enforce an arbitration clause can be brought under section 37(1) of the Senior Courts Act 1981 but concluded (consistently with the approach taken in *Starlight Shipping Co v Tai Ping Insurance Co Ltd (The Alexandros T)* [2008] 1 Lloyds Rep 230) that in doing so the court ought to have regard to the requirements of section 44 of the Arbitration Act 1996. However, this may not be the right analysis. It would clearly be inappropriate to convert the requirements of section 44 into rigid criteria rather than merely relevant factors in the exercise of the court's discretion. Further, in many of the reported cases the concepts deployed in section 44 have been ignored, without any obvious injustice. It may well be that the better approach would be to ignore the criteria in section 44 in this context, and replace them with a general discretionary principle that due regard should be given to whether it would not be more appropriate in the circumstances for the relevant remedies to be sought from the arbitrators themselves, at least in the first instance.

In *AES UST-Kamenogorsk Hydropower Plant LLP v UST-Kamenogorsk Hydropower Plant JSC* [2010] EHC 772, Burton J accepted that anti-suit injunctions to enforce an arbitration clause can be granted under section 37(1), without making any reference to the section 44 criteria: §19(ii)–(iii), 20. However, he made clear that in the light of section 1(c) of the 1996 Act, the Court would have to take great care not to usurp the arbitral process: at §21.

13.09 The recent authorities have not adopted Colman J's reasoning in *Sokana Industries v Freyre* [1994] 2 Lloyds Rep 57 (which appears to have been largely forgotten and is not generally cited) and instead proceed on the basis (which it is submitted is correct) that interim anti-suit injunctions to enforce an arbitration clause can in principle be granted under either section 44 of the Arbitration Act 1996 or section 37(1) of the Senior Courts Act 1981: see *Shashoua v Sharma* [2009] 2 Lloyds Rep 376, §§1–2; *Sheffield United FC Ltd v West Ham United FC Plc* [2009] 1 Lloyds Rep 167, §31; *AES UST-Kamenogorsk Hydropower Plant LLP v UST-Kamenogorsk Hydropower Plant JSC* [2010] EHC 772, §§18–20.

FN 22. However, section 44 does not apply in respect of ICSID arbitrations: *ETI Euro Telecom International BV v Republic of Bolivia* [2009] 1 WLR 665, §35. **13.10**

FN 27. In *ETI Euro Telecom International BV v Republic of Bolivia* [2009] 1 WLR 665, §§70–78, the Court of Appeal held that section 25(1) only gives power to the English courts to grant interim remedies in respect of substantive foreign court proceedings, and gives no power to grant interim remedies in support of foreign interim proceedings. **13.12**

FN 28. The proposition that section 25(1) gives no power to grant interim relief in support of foreign arbitration proceedings was confirmed in *ETI Euro Telecom International BV v Republic of Bolivia* [2009] 1 WLR 665, §§79–92.

D. THE PRINCIPLES TO BE APPLIED TO THE GRANT OF INTERIM ANTI-SUIT INJUNCTIONS

In *Sheffield United FC Ltd v West Ham United FC Plc* [2009] 1 Lloyds Rep 167, §§8–10, 21, the analysis of the authorities in these paragraphs of the original work was referred to and relied on by Teare J (who by error took the General Editor's name in vain in doing so). But Teare J did not need to decide which threshold test was the appropriate test as a matter of law. **13.27–13.29**

In addition, Teare J may have misinterpreted the suggestion in the original work that the threshold test was that the applicant must show that he is 'actually entitled to anti-suit relief' at the interim hearing. He viewed this as requiring that the applicant must show that he would be 'actually entitled' to relief at a final trial (see §21).

However, it is suggested that the approach which better reflects the existing authorities, and principle, is that on an interim application for an anti-suit injunction, where the facts are sufficiently clear, the court should not engage in assessing the level of probability (or certainty) that a *final* anti-suit injunction *would be granted at trial*, but instead should simply judge *whether the applicant is actually entitled to the anti-suit relief sought at the interim stage*. In this regard, the interim anti-suit injunction resembles a purely interim injunction such as a freezing injunction. (Where important facts are contested, the position may well be different, and it may well be required to prove those facts to some relevant threshold, such as a 'high degree of probability': see text to FN 75.)

It follows that Teare J's consideration of the 'balance of convenience', at §§24–29, might better have been pigeonholed as factors relevant to the court's discretion.

13.27 FN 62. See eg *Transfield Shipping Inc v Chiping Xinfa Huayu Alumina Co Ltd* [2009] EWHC 3629 (QB), §§52–54.

13.28 See *contra Rimpacific Navigation Inc v Daehan Shipbuilding Co Ltd (The Jin Man)* [2009] EWHC 2941 (Comm), §67, where without citation of authority David Steel J proceeded on the basis that it was sufficient if the injunction claimant could show there was a 'strongly arguable' case that its case on the existence of the jurisdiction clause was well founded. It is suggested that the analysis in the text remains the better statement of the law.

13.29 FNs 72 and 75. This is consistent with the approach taken in *Midgulf International Ltd v Groupe Chimiche Tunisien* [2009] 2 Lloyds Rep 411, §36. See further the discussion of *Sheffield United FC Ltd v West Ham United FC Plc* [2009] 1 Lloyds Rep 167, §§8–10, 21, at §§13.27–13.29 of this Supplement above.

13.31 FN 80. A different approach was taken in *Sheffield United FC Ltd v West Ham United FC Plc* [2009] 1 Lloyds Rep 167, §§9–10, 21, but it is submitted that the approach in the original text of this work is to be preferred. See further the comments under §§13.27–13.29 of this Supplement above.

13.32 FN 83. The approach proposed in the text was the view taken by Christopher Clarke J in *Transfield Shipping Inc v Chiping Xinfa Huayu Alumina Co Ltd* [2009] EWHC 3629 (QB), §§52–53. The learned judge observed that:

> it is only where the English court can point with confidence to a contractual promise not to litigate elsewhere that it can be justified in interfering with a party's right to bring its claim in such other place as might accept jurisdiction

a proposition that is correct, if confined (as it was intended to be confined) to contractual injunctions.

In *Rimpacific Navigation Inc v Daehan Shipbuilding Co Ltd (The Jin Man)* [2009] EWHC 2941, §67, David Steel J considered it was sufficient if the injunction claimant could show there was a 'strongly arguable' case that its case on the existence of the jurisdiction clause was well founded. There is little material difference between this approach and the propositions in the text, and David Steel J did not have the benefit of citation of the previous authorities.

13.34 FN 89. In *Midgulf International Ltd v Groupe Chimiche Tunisien* [2009] 2 Lloyds Rep 411, Teare J would have refused the interim anti-suit injunction, applying the general tests identified in §§13.27–13.29 of the original text of this work, because the claimant had not established a 'high degree of probability' that its case on the incorporation of an arbitration clause was correct (§§36, 39). Nevertheless, having ordered a speedy trial of that question, Teare J was willing, on the balance of convenience, to continue the interim injunction until after the determination of the trial (§43).

For recent examples of *Hemain* injunctions, see the mentions at *A v L* [2010] EWHC 460 (Fam), §14 and *JKN v JCN* [2010] EWHC 843 (Fam). **13.36**

FN 96. For a recent example of this, see *JKN v JCN* [2010] EWHC 843 (Fam), §32.

E. THE COURT'S DISCRETION

FN 98. For an example of an application for an interim anti-suit injunction dismissed on grounds of delay, see *Transfield Shipping Inc v Chiping Xinfa Huayu Alumina Co Ltd* [2009] EWHC 3629 (QB), §§71–79. **13.37**

FN 99. An application for an anti-suit injunction was dismissed because it was brought prematurely in *Hospira UK Ltd v Eli Lilly & Company* [2008] EWHC 1862 (Pat), §§11–13, where the defendant had not even threatened to bring proceedings, but had merely reserved its rights to do so.

FN 101. See *Sheffield United FC Ltd v West Ham United FC Plc* [2009] 1 Lloyds Rep 167, §22.

F. MANDATORY INTERIM INJUNCTIONS

FN 103. Mandatory interim injunctions were granted requiring the injunction defendant to release vessels from ship arrests abroad in *Kallang Shipping SA Panama v Axa Assurances Senegal (The Kallang) (No 2)* [2009] 1 Lloyds Rep 124, §§20–26; and *Sotrade Denizcilik Sanayi Ve Ticaret AS v Amadou Lo (The Duden)* [2009] 1 Lloyds Rep 145, §§23–29. **13.39**

14
Claims for Damages

A. DAMAGES FOR BREACH OF CONTRACT

Last sentence: in *CMA CGM v Hyundai MIPO Dockyard Co Ltd* [2009] 1 Lloyds Rep 213 Burton J held that a foreign *res judicata* would not preclude the ability to claim damages for breach of the forum clause; but this conclusion is doubtful. See §14.11 of this Supplement below. **14.01**

FN 1. In *Starlight Shipping Co v Tai Ping Insurance Co Ltd (The Alexandros T)* [2008] 1 Lloyd Rep 230, §12, Cooke J observed:

> Damages would, for all the reasons given in the authorities, be an inadequate remedy for breach of such a clause since its very nature requires the parties to have their disputes determined in arbitration. A party to such an agreement should not be put to the trouble of having disputes determined elsewhere in a manner contrary to the express contract between the parties.

It follows from this that damages are necessarily an inadequate remedy for breach of an exclusive forum clause in all or almost all circumstances, a conclusion adopted by Teare J in *Sheffield United FC Ltd v West Ham United FC Plc* [2009] 1 Lloyds Rep 167, §§22–23. See also *Steamship Mutual Underwriting Association (Bermuda) Ltd v Sulpicio Lines Inc* [2008] 2 Lloyds Rep 269, §32 (a decision reached at an undefended hearing).

In *Kallang Shipping SA Panama v Axa Assurances Senegal (The Kallang) (No 2)* [2009] 1 Lloyds Rep 124, the court held that maintaining foreign ship arrest proceedings for illegitimate purposes was a breach of an arbitration clause. The arrest had caused delay to the vessel. Jonathan Hirst QC concluded that even a legitimate arrest (that is, one that was sought only to obtain reasonable security), would have caused some delay but awarded damages for the extra period of delay caused by the illegitimate maintaining of the arrest, including damages for loss of hire, extra bunker consumption, and extra port **14.02** charges and fees (§§97–101). A similar analysis was adopted by the same judge in *Sotrade Denizcilik Sanayi Ve Ticaret AS v Amadou Lo (The Duden)* [2009] 1 Lloyds Rep 145, §§72–79. There appears to have been no argument that commercial losses of this nature should not be recoverable in principle.

For an earlier example of a claim for consequential financial losses, see *Ellerman Lines v Landi (The Falernian)* (1927) 29 Ll L Rep 15, 22–24, overturned in part on appeal *Ellerman Lines v Read* [1928] 2 KB 144 (CA), 153–154, 156–157, where the defendant had brought successful foreign ship arrest proceedings, which were in breach of contract and also involved a fraud. The claimant recovered damages for tug and crew expenses as a result of the arrest, legal expenses incurred in an attempt to obtain the ship's release, and the value of the ship which had been lost due to the arrest. However, the courts drew no distinction between damages recoverable as a result of the breach of contract, and damages recoverable for fraud.

For doubts as to whether it is correct, in principle, to treat an exclusive forum clause like other contractual obligations for the purposes of founding claims for damages, see J Harris, 'Agreements on jurisdiction and choice of law: where next?' [2009] LMCLQ 537, 548.

14.05 In respect of the possibility of a 'top-up' claim for the difference, see the discussion in A Briggs, *Agreements on Jurisdiction and Choice of Law* (OUP, 2008), §§8.18–8.21, where Professor Briggs suggests that the merger in judgment rule in Civil Jurisdiction and Judgments Act 1982, section 34, should not prevent a claim for a 'top-up'.

14.06 In *Kallang Shipping SA Panama v Axa Assurances Senegal (The Kallang) (No 2)* [2009] 1 Lloyds Rep 124, damages were claimed for legal costs incurred in Senegal incurred in successfully lifting an arrest, which the court had found had been legitimately obtained, but subsequently maintained in breach of contract. The claim for these legal costs was rejected on the ground that they would have been incurred even in lifting an arrest which had not been illegitimately maintained. There was no evidence as to the foreign court's costs rules and it seems that there was no argument of public policy against the recovery of such costs by way of damages.

14.07 In *Ellerman Lines v Landi (The Falernian)* (1927) 29 Ll L Rep 15, 22–23, damages were sought in respect of Turkish arrest proceedings which were in breach of contract and also involved a fraud on the Turkish court. Mackinnon J rejected the conclusion that the Turkish judgment *in rem* created any *res judicata* against the claimant in England, on a number of grounds, including lack of identity of parties, and no decision on the same issue. The argument that comity should preclude the grant of damages was not raised. These issues were not tested on appeal in *Ellerman Lines v*

Read [1928] 2 KB 144 (CA). See the discussion in A Briggs, *Agreements on Jurisdiction and Choice of Law* (OUP, 2008), §§8.05–8.06.

See also *Ellerman Lines v Landi (The Falernian)* (1927) 29 Ll L Rep 15, 22–23, where damages for legal expenses of an unsuccessful defence were awarded (not raised on appeal in *Ellerman Lines v Read* [1928] 2 KB 144 (CA)). However, in that case the foreign proceedings were not only in breach of contract but also involved a fraud on the foreign court. **14.08**

See A Briggs, *Agreements on Jurisdiction and Choice of Law* (OUP, 2008), §§8.13–8.14, 8.41–8.44, 8.58. **14.10**

However, a different view was taken by Burton J in *CMA CGM v Hyundai MIPO Dockyard Co Ltd* [2009] 1 Lloyds Rep 213, §§37–40. The learned judge concluded that, when assessing damages for breach of an exclusive forum clause, the relevant question is to ask what hypothetically the chosen forum would have held had the exclusive forum clause not been breached. In that hypothetical situation, there would have been no foreign judgment, and consequently, the fact that there now is a foreign judgment rejecting the damages claimant's substantive claims on the merits, which is arguably enforceable in England, is entirely irrelevant to the correct assessment of damages. Further, the damages claimant cannot be entitled to profit from its own wrong by relying on the foreign judgment reached in breach of the exclusive forum clause. Burton J therefore felt it was unnecessary for him to decide whether a Brussels–Lugano judgment reached in breach of an arbitration clause had to be recognized and enforced by English arbitrators (§41). **14.11**

However, it is submitted that Burton J was wrong in this regard. He was not referred to the earlier comments to the contrary of Hobhouse J in *Marc Rich & Co v Società Italiana Impianti (No 2)* (Hobhouse J, 11 November 1991). Further, as a matter of principle, his conclusion appears to understate the force of *res judicata* at common law and also the force of recognition under the Brussels–Lugano regime. The relevant estoppel is not a cause of action estoppel, but an issue estoppel. The effect of an *estoppel per rem judicatam* is to prevent the person estopped from arguing the contrary of the point which has already been decided. To make good the damages claim it is necessary to show that the damages claimant was right, and therefore would have succeeded on the merits in the proper forum. But if it has already been decided by a judgment requiring enforcement in England that the damages claimant was wrong on the merits of the underlying litigation, then the effect of the *estoppel per rem judicatam* is that the damages claimant cannot argue that he was right on the merits, and cannot therefore argue that he would hypothetically have been successful before the chosen forum (see the doubts of the Court of Appeal about Burton J's reasoning in *National Navigation Co v Endesa Generacion SA (The Wadi Sudr)* [2010] 1 Lloyds Rep 193 (CA), §56, and also at §118). The fallacy of Burton J's reasoning is to treat as decisive the question whether counterfactually there would have been a foreign judgment had the exclusive forum clause been respected, which there would not have been. This, however, is to start from the wrong starting point. Since there has been a foreign judgment, the *res judicata* is not a hypothetical possibility but an actuality, and thus an existing binding obligation. The counterfactual reasoning has to start on the basis of that binding obligation and assume it is correct, and consequently cannot ignore it or the foreign judgment.

As a result, it is submitted that if a damages claim for breach of an exclusive forum clause in respect of legal liabilities is to be viable, the question of whether the foreign judgment is to be enforced in England is inescapable and central and cannot be dismissed as an irrelevance.

In *Ellerman Lines v Landi (The Falernian)* (1927) 29 Ll L Rep 15, 22–23, the argument that the Turkish judgment was *res judicata* was rejected on more conventional grounds which are not of general application, namely lack of identity of parties, and no decision on the same issue. The point was not addressed on appeal in *Ellerman Lines Ltd v Read* [1928] 2 KB 144 (CA).

For a general discussion of the various possibilities in respect of *res judicata*, see A Briggs, *Agreements on Jurisdiction and Choice of Law* (OUP, 2008), §§8.15–8.46.

B. DAMAGES OUTSIDE THE CONTRACTUAL CASE

14.15 Choice of law points were not argued in *Kallang Shipping SA Panama v Axa Assurances Senegal (The Kallang) (No 2)* [2009] 1 Lloyds Rep 124, §§90–94 or *Sotrade Denizcilik Sanayi Ve Ticaret AS v Amadou Lo (The Duden)* [2009] 1 Lloyds Rep 145, §§65–70. See §14.18 of this Supplement below.

The Rome II Regulation is now in force.

14.17 FN 55. The rule that, in order to establish the tort of malicious prosecution, the foreign proceedings must have failed, applies only to substantive foreign proceedings which involve an examination of the factual merits, and not to *ex parte* applications or attachments: *Congentra AG v Sixteen Thirteen Marine SA (The Nicholas M)* [2008] 2 Lloyds Rep 602, §§38–44.

FN 56. In *Land Securities Ltd v Fladgate Fielder* [2010] 2 WLR 1265 (CA), the Court of Appeal held that there was no general tort of abuse of civil process, but only defined and limited instances of liability. But for a slightly more flexible approach, recognizing the possibility of a tort of wrongful attachment and of incremental development of the categories of liability, see *Congentra AG v Sixteen Thirteen Marine SA (The Nicholas M)* [2008] 2 Lloyds Rep 602, §§20–23.

In *Kallang Shipping SA Panama v Axa Assurances Senegal (The Kallang) (No 2)* [2009] 1 Lloyds Rep 124, §§90–94, where Axa Senegal had induced their insureds to breach an arbitration clause by orchestrating proceedings before the Courts of Senegal, Jonathan Hirst QC, sitting as a deputy judge, awarded damages against Axa Senegal for procuring a breach of contract. He observed that an alternative claim for interference in business relations by unlawful means added nothing (§94). A conspiracy claim was rejected on the grounds that Axa Senegal controlled the running of the case exclusively and so did not conspire with its insured in any meaningful sense (§96). However, as Jonathan Hirst QC stressed, both parties agreed that this issue was to be determined in accordance with English law and no case on Senegalese law was pleaded. In *Sotrade Denizcilik Sanayi Ve Ticaret AS v Amadou Lo (The Duden)* [2009] 1 Lloyds Rep 145, §§65–70, the same judge adopted the same analysis. **14.18**

The Rome II Regulation is now in force.

In *CMA CGM v Hyundai MIPO Dockyard Co Ltd* [2009] 1 Lloyds Rep 213, damages were awarded by an arbitration tribunal in respect of the pursuit of French court proceedings which the tribunal had held were in breach of the arbitration clause, and this award was upheld on appeal. It was not argued that it was in contrary to the principle of mutual trust for the arbitrators to award such damages, because the argument focussed on other issues, namely whether the arbitrators were bound by the *res judicata* effect of the French judgments. **14.22**

D. PERSONAL JURISDICTION

Old CPR 6.20(5) and 6.20(8) have now been replaced by new CPR 6.36 and PD 6B §3.1(6) and (9). Old CPR 6.19 is now replaced by new CPR 6.33. **14.23**

FN 85. The conclusion that claims for damages for breach of an arbitration clause will fall within the arbitration exception is supported by the Euorpean Court of Justice's decision in C-195/07, *Allianz AG v West Tankers Inc* [2009] ECR I-663, §§22–23.

15
Alternative Remedies

B. DECLARATIONS

FN 3. A declaration of this type was granted by Gloster J in *National Navigation Co v Endesa Generacion SA (The Wadi Sudr)* [2009] 1 Lloyds Rep 666, §§74, 127. The judge's decision was overturned on appeal, but on the separate ground that a contrary prior Spanish court decision should be recognized in England: see [2010] 1 Lloyds Rep 193 (CA), §133. **15.03**

The argument that a claim for a declaration that an arbitration clause had been validly incorporated into a contract was impermissible, where no arbitration had actually been commenced and none was intended to be commenced by the party seeking to enforce the arbitration clause, was rejected by Burton J in *AES UST-Kamenogorsk Hydropower Plant LLP v UST-Kamenogorsk Hydropower JSC* [2010] EWHC 772 (Comm), §§18–19, 21–22. Burton J concluded that such a declaration would not infringe the principle of non-intervention in arbitrations enshrined in section 1(c) of the Arbitration Act 1996. He declined to follow the contrary reasoning of Thomas J in the earlier case of *Vale do Rio Doce Navegaçao SA v Shanghai Bao Steel Ocean Shipping Co Ltd* [2000] 2 Lloyds Rep 1, §§51–54. However, Burton J confined his decision to the case where a party wished to be sued only in arbitration if at all, and did not itself wish to commence an arbitration. He left open the possibility that (as Thomas J had held), if the party seeking the declaration as to the enforceability of the arbitration clause himself wished to arbitrate and was going to commence or had commenced arbitration proceedings, then his appropriate course was to seek relief from the arbitrators (or under section 32 of the Arbitration Act 1996) and not by way of a claim for a declaration. **15.04**

In *AES UST-Kamenogorsk Hydropower Plant LLP v UST-Kamenogorsk Hydropower JSC* [2010] EWHC 772 (Comm), §§18–19, 21–22, Burton J did **15.06** not follow *Vale do Rio Doce Navegaçao SA v Shanghai Bao Steel Ocean Shipping Co Ltd* in this regard: see §15.04 of this Supplement.

15.07 In *AES UST-Kamenogorsk Hydropower Plant LLP v UST-Kamenogorsk Hydropower JSC* [2010] EWHC 772 (Comm), §§18(vi) and 22, Burton J misunderstood the reference to *'the court's existing practice'* in this paragraph of the original text, which was intended to refer to the common practice of granting declarations that arbitration clauses were binding irrespective of the problems raised by section 32 and section 1(c) of the 1996 Act.

Burton J in any event concluded (see the discussion at §15.04 above) that a party who did not wish to arbitrate, but contended that any claim against him should be arbitrated, and wished to obtain a declaration to ensure that if he was sued at all, that suit should be advanced in arbitration, would be entitled to seek a declaration from the court as to the binding force of the arbitration agreement. He therefore departed from the decision of Thomas J in *Vale do Rio Doce Navegaçao SA v Shanghai Bao Steel Ocean Shipping Co Ltd* [2000] 2 Lloyds Rep 1, §§51–54 to that extent, but expressly did not decide whether a declaration should also be possible where the declaration claimant did in fact wish to arbitrate.

It is respectfully suggested that Burton J's conclusion is correct so far as it goes, and that it should be developed further, to apply to all cases of declarations as to the binding force of arbitration agreements. The decisions of Clarke J in *ABB Lummus Global Ltd v Keppel Fels Ltd* [1999] 2 Lloyds Rep 24, and Thomas J in *Vale Do Rio*, where they held that section 32 of the Arbitration Act 1996 should be the exclusive route by which declarations as to the binding force of arbitration clauses should be brought before the Court, are not logically inevitable. They would also produce impractical consequences, because of the delay which would be involved in appointing a tribunal before section 32 could be engaged (as mentioned in the main text of this work).

The inconvenient effects of delay are now all the more important after the decision of the Court of Appeal in *National Navigation Co v Endesa Generacion SA (The Wadi Sudr)* [2010] 1 Lloyds Rep 193 (CA), where it was held that breach of an English arbitration clause was not a reason to refuse recognition of a Brussels–Lugano judgment in England. It seems to follow that the *only* technique available to protect an English arbitration clause, which under English law and principles of private international law would be treated as valid, from being overridden by the law of another Brussels–Lugano state, is to obtain a prior declaration from the English courts (or a prior award from the arbitrators) as to its validity: see §§15.21 and 15.29 of this Supplement. But if so, the speed with which such declarations could be obtained could become decisive.

In addition, the distinction which Burton J's decision in *AES UST* leaves open, between situations where the declaration claimant did not intend to commence an arbitration and situations where that was his intention, would be unsustainable in practice and would lead to abuse.

Consequently, it is submitted that the general exclusionary principle articulated in *Vale do Rio* should no longer be treated as the law. Declarations as to the validity and binding force of arbitration clauses should be permissible, in the court's discretion, where the operation of the normal processes of allowing the tribunal to rule on its jurisdiction under sections 30–31 of the 1996 Act, or obtaining a preliminary ruling from the court with the tribunal's consent under section 32 of the 1996 Act, would not be appropriate or expedient. As the court's existing practice shows, it will often be appropriate and expedient to grant a declaration (outside section 32) where competing court proceedings have been brought abroad which are inconsistent with the arbitration clause.

For other examples of declarations of this nature being granted, see *Steamship Mutual Underwriting Association (Bermuda) Ltd v Sulpicio Lines Inc* [2008] 2 Lloyds Rep 269, §34 (a decision reached at an uncontested hearing), and also *National Navigation Co v Endesa Generacion SA (The Wadi Sudr)* [2009] 1 Lloyds Rep 666, §§74, 127 (result overturned on appeal, but solely because it was held that a contrary prior Spanish court decision should be recognized in England: see [2010] 1 Lloyds Rep 193 (CA), §133).

Old CPR 6.20(5)(c) and (d) are now new CPR 6.36 and PD 6B §3.1(6)(c) and (d). **15.08**

FN 22. In *Underwriting Members of Lloyd's Syndicate 980 v Sinco SA* [2009] ILPr 49, a Greek claim for tort damages in relation to the substantive dispute had been brought first in Greece inconsistently with the terms of the alleged jurisdiction clause. The defendant in Greece brought before the English courts a claim for damages for the breach of the exclusive jurisdiction clause which it was alleged that the Greek action constituted. Beatson J concluded that the English claim did not have the same 'cause of action' as the Greek action. However, he allowed for the possibility that an English action, including a claim for damages of this kind, might involve the 'same cause of action', if it was the 'mirror image' of the foreign action. On the facts before him, he did not need to determine whether the analytical approach in *Evialis v SEAT* or the different approach in *Continental Bank v Aeakos* (Gatehouse J), and the two *Toepfer* decisions, was correct. But he indicated that he did not think that *Aeakos* and the two *Toepfer* decisions were wrong. In the circumstances, although Beatson J's decision only directly concerned a claim for damages, it supports the conclusion that a **15.09** claim for a declaration as to the binding effect of a jurisdiction clause will not be caught by Article 27 due to the existence of prior foreign proceedings on the merits, unless the nature of the prior foreign proceedings is such that they can be seen as a mirror image of the claim in England (for example, if there is a claim for a negative declaration as to the non-existence of the jurisdiction clause in the foreign proceedings).

FN 23. The conclusion that the English declaration claim as to the validity of an exclusive jurisdiction clause should not be stayed under Article 28, at least where the claim is a strong one, is supported by *JP Morgan v Primacom* [2005] 2 Lloyds Rep 665, where Cooke J concluded (in a case which was not concerned with a declaration as to the effect of an exclusive jurisdiction clause) that if the court was of the view that the foreign proceedings were in breach of an exclusive jurisdiction clause, that was a strong reason why Article 28 should not be engaged in respect of related English proceedings: 'The injustice of giving precedence to proceedings in breach of an exclusive jurisdiction clause where the parties have agreed that England is the appropriate forum is self-evident.'

15.10 FN 24. This is now clear beyond doubt in the light of C-195/07, *Allianz v West Tankers Inc (The Front Comor)* [2009] ECR I-663, §§22–23 and *National Navigation Co v Endesa Generacion SA (The Wadi Sudr)* [2009] 1 Lloyds Rep 666, §§74, 127 (overturned, but not on this point, in CA).

Text to FN 25. Old CPR 6.20(5)(c) is now new CPR 6.36 and PD 6B §3.1(6)(c).

15.11 FN 27. See further, in this context, *CMA CGM v Hyundai MIPO Dockyard Co Ltd* [2009] 1 Lloyds Rep 213, §§35–36, 41–47 where the arbitrators had concluded that they were not bound by the Brussels–Lugano regime at all. On appeal Burton J indicated that he was sympathetic to the Tribunal's approach, but did not need to decide the point as he upheld the award on other grounds. In *National Navigation Co v Endesa Generacion SA (The Wadi Sudr)* [2010] 1 Lloyds Rep 193 (CA), the Court of Appeal disagreed with aspects of Burton J's reasoning on this question, so far as concerns the arbitrators' obligation to obey *res judicata*, but not in such a way as to affect the conclusion on this point.

15.16 FN 34. This issue was commented on in a glancing fashion in *DHL v Fallimento Finmatica* [2009] 1 Lloyds Rep 430, §23.

D. PROCEDURAL MANAGEMENT

15.20 Text and notes to FN 43. This conclusion was assumed to be correct, *obiter*, by Waller LJ in *National Navigation Co v Endesa Generacion SA (The Wadi*

Sudr) [2010] 1 Lloyds Rep 193 (CA), §§6, 41–42, 63. However, it is to be noted that (i) Waller LJ may have been of the view that; (ii) only an arbitration award on the merits, rather than merely on the validity of the arbitration agreement, would preclude the recognition of a subsequent Brussels–Lugano judgment on the merits (at §63); (iii) in Waller LJ's opinion, the non-recognition of the subsequent inconsistent Brussels–Lugano judgment could only be defended under Article 34(3), and not on the basis of public policy (§§64–65). Moore-Bick LJ did not address these issues.

The Court of Appeal has now concluded, in *National Navigation Co v Endesa Generacion SA (The Wadi Sudr)* [2010] 1 Lloyds Rep 193 (CA), that a judgment of another Brussels–Lugano court ruling that an arbitration clause is invalid should be enforced in England, at least in most cases, even if that judgment was obtained in breach of an arbitration clause which is valid from an English perspective. Given that anti-suit injunctions to restrain Brussels–Lugano proceedings brought in breach of arbitration clauses are also now prohibited following *Allianz AG v West Tankers Inc (The Front Comor)*, the net result is that winning the litigation race, and obtaining a prior *res judicata* from the English courts (or a prior abitration award) to the effect that the arbitration clause *is* binding, may be the *only* effective way of defending an English arbitration clause by proceedings in England. **15.21**

E. RESISTING ENFORCEMENT

The possibilities of resisting enforcement are in any event more limited now in the light of the Court of Appeal's decision in *National Navigation Co v Endesa Generacion SA (The Wadi Sudr)* [2010] 1 Lloyds Rep 193 (CA), discussed at §15.29 of this Supplement below. **15.26**

Text to FN 56. This conclusion follows *a fortiori* from the Court of Appeal's reasoning in *National Navigation Co v Endesa Generacion SA (The Wadi Sudr)* [2010] 1 Lloyds Rep 193 (CA). **15.28**

FN 57. The public policy argument in this regard, raised by Waller J in *Bamberger*, is now inconsistent with the narrower approach to public policy in *National Navigation Co v Endesa Generacion SA (The Wadi Sudr)* [2010] 1 Lloyds Rep 193 (CA), §§63–65.

FN 58. However, the *lis pendens* problem now appears to be diminished at least on the current approach being taken by the English courts: see

Underwriting Members of Lloyd's Syndicate 980 v Sinco SA [2009] ILPr 49, discussed at §15.22 of this Supplement above.

15.29 FNs 60 and 61.

(a) It is clear, at least for now, that a judgment of another Brussels–Lugano court obtained in breach of an arbitration agreement (which would be valid from an English perspective) must be recognized and enforced in England, even to the extent that it contains a ruling as to the invalidity of the arbitration clause: C-195/07, *Allianz v West Tankers Inc (The Front Comor)* [2009] ECR I-663, as interpreted in *National Navigation Co v Endesa Generacion SA (The Wadi Sudr)* [2010] 1 Lloyds Rep 193 (CA). The previous first instance decisions and opinions to the contrary in England have therefore been overruled (thus the recent decisions in *CMA CGM v Hyundai MIPO Dockyard Co Ltd* [2009] 1 Lloyds Rep 213, §§35–35, 41–47 and *National Navigation Co v Endesa Generacion SA (The Wadi Sudr)* [2009] 1 Lloyds Rep 666, §§74, 127 are no longer good law).

(b) Further, such a Brussels–Lugano judgment must be recognized not only by the English courts but also by an English arbitration tribunal: *National Navigation Co v Endesa Generacion SA (The Wadi Sudr)* [2010] 1 Lloyds Rep 193 (CA), §§56, 118–119, 123.

(c) This result was arrived at in an unsatisfactory way, and produces deeply unsatisfactory results. The problem arises because the European Court of Justice concluded in *The Front Comor* that a Brussels–Lugano court's decision that an arbitration clause was invalid, if reached in the context of proceedings on the merits which themselves fell within the scope of the Brussels–Lugano regime, was a preliminary matter in the substantive litigation and therefore itself also within the scope of the Brussels–Lugano regime (at §§26–27). But this was an unnecessary side effect of the European Court of Justice's determination to condemn anti-suit injunctions to enforce an arbitration clause (discussed further at Ch 12, §§12.15–12.27 of this Supplement).

(d) The European Court of Justice could have concluded that such anti-suit injunctions were prohibited by the principle of mutual trust, because it was for the other Brussels–Lugano court to decide whether or not it should exercise its *putative* Brussels–Lugano jurisdiction on the merits, without deciding that the other court's decision that the arbitration clause was valid or invalid was itself within the scope of the regime. There is little sign in the European Court of Justice's brief reasoning that the gravity of the collateral decision it was taking was fully appreciated, and its consideration of the previous authorities and literature was inadequate. Notably, its reliance on the (not particularly authoritative) Evrigenis and Kerameus report in this regard (at §27), while ignoring the doubts of the Schlosser report (at §62) and the contrary views of Advocate General Darmon in *Marc Rich & Co AG v Società Italiana Impianti SpA (The Atlantic Emperor)* [1991] ECR I-3855, AG §45, leaves much to be desired. The weakness of the European Court of Justice's reasoning was commented on by Gloster J in *National Navigation Co v Endesa Generacion SA (The Wadi Sudr)* [2009] 1 Lloyds Rep 666, §89.

(e) There was potentially some room to argue that the European Court of Justice's comments in this regard should be treated as *obiter dicta* and as not having binding force in the context of enforcement and recognition but neither Gloster J nor the Court of Appeal in *The Wadi Sudr* accepted that argument, considering that it was clear that the European Court of Justice had indeed ruled that the other Brussels–Lugano court's decision on the validity or invalidity of the arbitration clause was within the scope of the Brussels–Lugano regime for all purposes: *National Navigation Co v Endesa Generacion SA (The Wadi Sudr)* [2009] 1 Lloyds Rep 666, §§88–90; [2010] 1 Lloyds Rep 193 (CA), §§32–46, 100. See also, to the same effect, *DHL v Fallimento Finmatica* [2009] 1 Lloyds Rep 430, §20.

(f) Gloster J nevertheless concluded that she was not bound to recognize the judgment of the Italian court holding that the arbitration clause was not incorporated, on the grounds that (i) as she was considering a matter that was outside the arbitration exception, she was not bound by the recognition and enforcement obligations of the Brussels–Lugano regime; (ii) in any event, to enforce a foreign judgment in breach of an English arbitration clause would be contrary to public policy, and consequently, recognition could be refused under Article 35(3) of the Brussels I Regulation: at §§91–97, 98–102. But the Court of Appeal concluded that neither line of reasoning was workable: at §§47–59, 60–67, 108–123, and 124–133.

(g) It should be noted the Court of Appeal's conclusion in respect of public policy may be dependent on the facts of the case. The Spanish court had refused to give effect to the incorporation of the arbitration clause in the bill of lading from the voyage charterparty, relying on the more restrictive, but apparently perfectly rational, Spanish law rules on incorporation. The Court of Appeal concluded that such a Spanish judgment, even though different to the decision an English court would have reached, was not such as to involve a manifest breach of English public policy. But Moore-Bick LJ left open the possibility that in other cases—for example where there is no defensible reason whatsoever for the foreign court to have not given effect to the arbitration clause, or where the foreign judgment had been obtained 'through conscious wrongdoing', a different conclusion might be reached (see at §§125, 131–132. On the other hand, Waller LJ's decision that public policy could not be relied on was reasoned in more absolute terms (see at §62); Carnwath LJ agreed with both judgments, so it is unclear which approach represents the law.

(h) The Court of Appeal was well aware that the answer reached was unsatisfactory in its effects, as Waller LJ expressly noted (at §41–42) that it produces a result

> which leaves the court in member state A where the proceedings on the merits have been commenced free to ignore a judgment in arbitration proceedings in state B the seat of the arbitration, but if a preliminary ruling can be obtained early enough in state A, the courts in state B are bound by the result of the preliminary ruling in state A.

But, with respect, the true implications of this decision are more serious even than the Court of Appeal allowed. It means that the arbitration-unfriendly domestic laws of other member states can be manipulated to override English arbitration law in England and in English arbitrations.

(i) It was precisely because of the dangers presented by the inconsistencies between national arbitration laws that the UK fought hard, during the negotiations for the UK's accession to the Brussels Convention, for this aspect of the interpretation of the arbitration exception to be clarified in favour of the opposite solution to that which the Court of Appeal has now adopted. The Schlosser Report, §§61–62, recorded the agreement of the negotiators that 'The new member states can deal with this problem of interpretation in their implementing legislation' and it is that possibility which the Court of Appeal has abandoned. So there is perhaps more force to the arguments based on public policy than the Court of Appeal allowed: the enforcement of the policies of English arbitration law in English arbitrations can defensibly be viewed as fundamental to the UK's legal order (to use the tests articulated by the ECJ in C-7/98, *Bamberski v Krombach* [2000] ECR I-1935).

(j) In addition, the Court of Appeal refused to accept that this result was inconsistent with the UK's obligations under the New York Convention. They held, in effect, that Article II-1 and II-3 of the New York Convention could be applied on the basis of the other Brussels–Lugano court's conclusion as to whether or not the arbitration clause was binding, which the English court was obliged to enforce (§§69, 127). But with respect, this reasoning may have started from the wrong end of the telescope. The better way to analyse the question may be to ask, first, whether English law regards an arbitration clause as void or incapable of being performed for the purposes of Article II-1 and II-3 (and receive the answer 'No'), *before* turning to the question of recognition and enforcement under the Brussels–Lugano regime. If, armed with that conclusion, one then turns to consider the effect of a Brussels–

Lugano judgment producing a different result, it is arguable that there is a clash between what are, in the first place, the UK's obligations under the New York Convention before the question of recognition under the Brussels–Lugano regime is introduced, and the obligations otherwise imposed by the Brussels–Lugano regime. If so, then there would be an argument that the UK is not obliged to recognize the judgment creating the clash, pursuant to Article 71 of the Brussels I Regulation (although this would require Article 71 to be interpreted in a purposive fashion, so that 'jurisdiction or recognition or enforcement of judgments' includes stays in favour of arbitration and the enforcement of arbitration awards).

(k) In conclusion, there are real reasons to doubt the correctness of both *The Front Comor* and *The Wadi Sudr*. Salvation, if any, will have to come either from the UK Supreme Court or the European Court of Justice or from European legislation. But there is a real prospect of reform at the European level. In the context of the ongoing review of the Brussels I Regulation, influential voices have been raised to argue for a reversal of *The Front Comor* in this regard. At the time of writing (10 June 2010) the current draft of the report being prepared by the European Parliament's Legal Affairs Committee specifically proposes that the Brussels I Regulation should be amended:

> so as to make it clear that proceedings brought in breach of arbitration clauses and judgments not given by the competent court holding that arbitration clauses are invalid fall outside of the scope of the Regulation and are therefore not enforceable in other Member States.

(l) See the critical discussion of the result reached by the Court of Appeal, if not their reasoning, in R Fentiman, 'Arbitration Agreements in Europe' [2010] CLJ 242; S Dutson, M Howarth, 'Dead ahead? West Tankers Sails on in the Court of Appeal in the Wadi Sudr', Arbitration 2010, 76(2), 374–385.

Text and notes to FN 62. In *National Navigation Co v Endesa Generacion SA (The Wadi Sudr)* [2010] 1 Lloyds Rep 193 (CA), §§6, 41–42, 63, Waller LJ accepted at least that (i) a prior declaration by the English court as to the validity of an arbitration clause would preclude enforcement of a Brussels–Lugano judgment holding that the arbitration clause was invalid; (ii) a prior arbitration award on the merits would preclude enforcement of an inconsistent Brussels–Lugano judgment on the merits reached in breach of the arbitration clause. However, he appeared to envisage (but did not directly address) that, if no arbitration award on the merits had been obtained, a prior Court declaration as to the validity of the arbitration clause would *not* preclude enforcement of a Brussels–Lugano judgment on the merits obtained in breach of the clause.

Text and notes to FN 63. The idea that an English arbitration tribunal (in contrast to an English court) might be entitled to refuse to enforce a Brussels–Lugano judgment reached in breach of an arbitration clause was adopted by the arbitrators, and mentioned with approval by Burton J, in *CMA CGM v Hyundai MIPO Dockyard Co Ltd* [2009] 1 Lloyds Rep 213, §§35–36, 45–46, 41–47. However, in *National Navigation Co v Endesa Generacion SA (The Wadi Sudr)* [2010] 1 Lloyds Rep 193 (CA), §§56, 118, the Court of Appeal disagreed (*obiter*), reasoning that a Brussels–Lugano judgment if recognized would create a *res judicata* which arbitrators would be obliged to respect.

FNs 65–67. In *National Navigation Co v Endesa Generacion SA (The Wadi Sudr)* [2010] 1 Lloyds Rep 193 (CA), §125, Moore-Bick LJ envisaged the possibility of a defence to recognition of a Brussels–Lugano judgment which had been reached by pursuing proceedings in defiance of an anti-suit injunction. But, as noted in the original text, it can be doubted whether such a refusal of recognition would be consistent with the Brussels–Lugano regime, given the hostility shown by the European Court to the principle of anti-suit injunctions.

In any event, following C-195/07, *Allianz v West Tankers Inc (The Front Comor)* [2009] ECR I-663, there will now be no cases where anti-suit injunctions can be granted to restrain the pursuit of proceedings within the material scope of the Brussels–Lugano regime before other Brussels–Lugano courts. There is still the possibility of anti-suit injunctions to restrain proceedings elsewhere in Europe which are outside the material scope of the Brussels–Lugano regime; but in such a case, any resultant judgment would not be a Brussels–Lugano judgment for the purposes of enforcement.

(In *Golubovich v Golubovich* [2010] EWCA Civ 810, the Court of Appeal recognized a Russian divorce judgment which had been obtained in breach of an anti-suit injunction. However, the decision turns on the special features of divorce judgments and is not generalizable outside family law.)

16

The Framework of Jurisdictional Law

B. THE FRAMEWORK OF ENGLISH JURISDICTIONAL LAW

FN 3. The New Lugano Convention has been ratified by the EU and Norway, and is now in force as between the EU and Norway with effect from 1 January 2010: see Civil Jurisdiction and Judgments Regulations 2009, SI 2009/3131. Pursuant to a decision of the Swiss Federal Council of 31 March 2010, Switzerland will ratify the Convention with effect from 1 January 2011. It has not yet been ratified by Iceland. **16.03**

FN 4. See now also Council Regulation (EC) 4/2009 on jurisdiction, applicable law, recognition and enforcement of decisions, and cooperation in matters relating to maintenance obligations.

Text at FN 5. Parallel provisions of the Regulation will be given a scope identical to the corresponding provisions of the Brussels Convention so as to ensure a uniform interpretation of the two instruments: C-533/07, *Falco Privatstiftung v Weller-Lindhorst* [2010] Bus LR 210, ECJ §§52, 53, 56.

C. THE MATERIAL SCOPE OF THE BRUSSELS–LUGANO REGIME

FN 16. See also A Rushworth, 'Demarcating the boundary between the Brussels I Regulation and the Evidence Regulation' [2009] LMCLQ 196, 204. **16.11**

In C-195/07, *Allianz AG v West Tankers Inc (The Front Comor)* [2009] ECR I-663, the European Court of Justice held that an anti-suit injunction to **16.12** enforce an arbitration clause fell within the 'arbitration' exception. However, it did so on the basis of two concepts, which it treated as congruent but are in fact different: (i) 'in order to determine whether a dispute falls within the scope of Regulation 44/2001, reference must be made solely to the subject matter of the proceedings' while (ii) 'More specifically its place in the scope of Regulation 44/2001 is determined by the nature of the rights which the proceedings in question serve to protect' (ECJ, §§22–23). (In contrast, the Advocate General had used one test only, namely that 'whether or not proceedings fall within the scope of the Convention or Regulation 44/2001 must therefore be determined from the substantive subject matter of the dispute': see AG §52.)

These two tests produce the same answer with relative clarity in relation to injunctions to enforce an arbitration clause, because in such a case, both the underlying proceedings, and the contractual right to insist on arbitration which justifies the injunction, can be seen as being 'arbitration'. But the same coincidence of juridical basis does not apply to anti-suit injunctions sought to protect substantive proceedings falling within the other exceptions to the scope of the Brussels–Lugano regime. For example, if an anti-suit injunction is sought to protect English insolvency proceedings, it will itself be based on equitable principles, and justified on the grounds that the foreign proceedings are vexatious and oppressive. Consequently, it remains unclear whether in such situations the 'rights' in question which the injunction is sought to protect would be viewed as the underlying substantive rights (which *ex hypothesi* are excluded from the scope of the Brussels–Lugano regime) or the equitable right to the injunction, which treated on its own probably falls within the scope of the Brussels–Lugano regime. In the circumstances, it is uncertain whether Lord Hoffmann's conclusion that anti-suit injunctions sought to protect substantive proceedings which fall outside the scope of the Brussels–Lugano regime will 'borrow' the characterization of the underlying proceedings does indeed represent the law in relation to the other exceptions to the material scope of Brussels–Lugano regime.

16.13 FN 28. In C-195/07, *Allianz AG v West Tankers Inc (The Front Comor)* [2009] ECR I-663, the European Court of Justice held that an anti-suit injunction to enforce an arbitration clause fell within the 'arbitration' exception and was thus outside the scope of the Brussels–Lugano regime (§§22–23). However, it insisted the grant of such injunctions to restrain the pursuit of proceedings before other Brussels–Lugano courts was nevertheless precluded by the principle of mutual trust.

Text to FN 29. The proposition in the main text remains the law. See Ch 12, §§12.10–12.12, of this Supplement.

17

Jurisdiction under the Brussels–Lugano Regime

A. INTRODUCTION

FNs 3 and 4. The conclusion that the principle of mutual trust between European Courts does not prevent the grant of anti-suit injunctions to restrain proceedings outside the Brussels–Lugano zone has been repeatedly re-affirmed by the English courts, and has received indirect support from the French Cour de Cassation. See the discussion at Ch 12, §§12.10–12.12 of this Supplement. This is also consistent with the reasoning of the European Court of Justice in C-195/07, *Allianz AG v West Tankers Inc (The Front Comor)* [2009] ECR I-663, which was based principally on the impermissibility of interfering with the right of a court of another European state from ruling on the exercise of its own Brussels–Lugano jurisdiction: see §§27, 29. **17.02**

FN 5. It follows from the European Court of Justice's decision in C-195/07, *Allianz v West Tankers Inc (The Front Comor)* [2009] ECR I-663, that the Brussels–Lugano regime has no preclusive jurisdictional effect on anti-suit injunctions to enforce arbitration clauses provided that they do not seek to restrain the pursuit of proceedings before another Brussels–Lugano court: see §§23–24.

B. JURISDICTION OVER FINAL ANTI-SUIT INJUNCTIONS UNDER THE BRUSSELS–LUGANO REGIME

17.09–17.12 In C-195/07, *Allianz AG v West Tankers Inc* [2009] ECR I-663, §§23–24, the European Court of Justice held that injunctions to enforce arbitration clauses were within the arbitration exception and thus outside the scope of the Brussels–Lugano regime. Although the Court concluded that such injunctions were impermissible, to the extent that they sought to restrain the pursuit of proceedings before other member state courts, this was a substantive and not a jurisdictional conclusion. It thus remains the law that Article 5(1) is irrelevant to, and cannot support jurisdiction over, claims to enforce an arbitration clause by anti-suit injunction or damages, as Gloster J held in *National Navigation Co v Endesa Generation SA (The Wadi Sudr)* [2009] 1 Lloyds Rep 666, §§69, a conclusion with which the Court of Appeal agreed [2010] 1 Lloyds Rep 193, §§26–27, 134–137.

In the circumstances, the counterfactual hypothesis on which the reasoning in §§17.10–17.12 of the main text explicitly proceeded does not arise and no longer needs to be addressed, as Gloster J recognized in *National Navigation Co v Endesa Generation SA (The Wadi Sudr)* [2009] 1 Lloyds Rep 666, §69.

17.13 As prefigured in FN 32 of the original text, the consequence of C-195/07, *Allianz v West Tankers Inc (The Front Comor)* [2009] ECR I-663, §§23–24, will now be that anti-suit injunctions to enforce arbitration clauses fall outside the Brussels–Lugano regime altogether, and cannot be justified under Article 5(1), even if the arbitration clause in question forms part of a contract for the sale of goods or the provision services.

17.16 FN 37. See also *Dexter v Harley* (Lloyd J, 8 March 2001, unreported), §13.

17.19 A difficult line of European Court of Justice authorities suggests that the requirement of a 'real issue to be tried' against the anchor defendant, laid down in *The Rewia*, may not be a condition of the application of Article 6(1): see C-98/06, *Freeport v Arnoldsson* [2007] ECR I-8319, §§49–54; *Reisch Montage AG v Kiesel Baumaschinen Handels Gmbh* [2006] ECR I-6827, §§27, 28, 31, 32 (inconsistent with *Freeport*, in particular at §32); C-426/06, *Glaxosmithkline v Rouard* [2008] ECR I-3965, §33. However, even if that is what the European Court of Justice really means, which the English courts will be disinclined to accept, it does not affect, and merely reinforces, the conclusion that Article 6(1) is available in principle to support claims for final anti-suit injunctions against co-defendants. Recent English decisions have followed the approach in *The Rewia*, but without the potential problem arising from the *Freeport* line of European Court of Justice authorities having been raised before the court.

FN 19. *Masri v Consolidated Contractors International Company SAL (No 3)* [2009] QB 503, §31, could be read as holding that even a claim for a final anti-suit injunction is not a claim for substantive relief. But it is submitted this is not the law: see §16.11 of the main text of this work.

For a general discussion of the purpose of the special regime for insurance in Section 3 of the Regulation, see C-347/08, *Vorarlberger Gebietskrankenkasse v WGV-Schwäbische Allgemeine Versicherungs AG* [2010] IL Pr 2 (ECJ), §§40–41. **17.30**

For confirmation that the scope of Article 22 should be interpreted restrictively, and thus probably will not apply to anti-suit injunctions even where England has exclusive jurisdiction over the substantive dispute, see C-343/04, *Land Oberösterreich v ČEZ AS* [2006] ECR I-4557, §34, where the European Court held that an action for nuisance did not come within Article 22, even though the basis of the action was an interference with real property, because 'the real and immovable nature of the right at issue does not have a decisive influence on the issues to be determined in the dispute in the main proceedings'. **17.33**

FN 67. See also *Hoddinott v Persimmon Homes (Wessex) Ltd* [2008] 1 WLR 806 (CA), §§26–29. **17.35**

For further confirmation that the Court has power to extend the relevant time limit, see *Sawyer v Atari Interactive Inc* [2006] ILPr 129, §§46–47; *Texan Management Limited v Pacific Electric Wire & Cable Company* [2009] UKPC Case Ref 46, §§73–74, 76.

C. *LIS PENDENS*

Text to FN 77. The conclusion in the main text has now been confirmed by C-195/07, *Allianz AG v West Tankers Inc (The Front Comor)* [2009] ECR I-663. **17.38**

FN 80. In *Underwriting Members of Lloyd's Syndicate 980 v Sinco SA* [2008] 2 CLC 187, a Greek claim for tort damages in relation to the substantive dispute had been brought first in Greece inconsistently with the terms of the alleged jurisdiction clause. The defendant in Greece brought before the English courts a claim for damages for the breach of the exclusive jurisdiction clause which it was alleged that the Greek action constituted. Beatson J concluded that the English claim did not have the same 'cause of **17.39** action' as the Greek action. However, he allowed for the possibility that an English action, including a claim for damages of this kind, might involve the 'same cause of action', if it was the 'mirror image' of the foreign action.

D. INTERIM ANTI-SUIT INJUNCTIONS

17.42 FN 88. In *Masri v Consolidated Contractors International Company SAL (No 4)* [2010] AC 90 (HL) (on appeal from *Masri v Toufic Khoury* [2008] EWCA Civ 625), the House of Lords upheld the appeal without needing to address the European law issues which arose, and so the scope of the parasitic jurisdiction as regards parties to proceedings was not considered. However, Lord Mance's reasoning is implicitly inconsistent with any conclusion that the 'parasitic jurisdiction' creates a power to bring non-parties before the court: see §§29–30.

17.43 FN 88. For discussion of the *Masri* litigation, see A Briggs, 'Enforcing and reinforcing an English judgment' [2008] LMCLQ 421.

17.45 Text and note at FN 95. CPR Part 6 has now been heavily rewritten, and the result is an apparent lacuna in the rules as to service out of the jurisdiction in cases governed by the Brussels–Lugano regime. New CPR 6.33 gives powers only to serve the 'claim form' out of the jurisdiction without the permission of the court, and the definition of 'claim form' in new CPR 6.2(c) includes only application notices in 'any application made before action or to commence proceedings'. The technique that was possible under the old rules, of including application notices within the primary heads of power for service out of the jurisdiction, is thus now oddly only possible for interim anti-suit injunctions sought before the commencement of proceedings. Further, new CPR 6.38(1) only makes express provision for what happens 'where the permission of the court is required for the claimant to serve the claim form out of the jurisdiction' and thus does not apply in Brussels–Lugano cases. However, it is inevitable that the English court will plug this gap (which in any event is only a problem in practice in the small number of cases where proceedings have been commenced but the injunction defendant has not given an address for service). Under the Brussels–Lugano regime, the rules as to service out of the jurisdiction do not define jurisdiction (in contrast to the position under the common law rules) but are instead merely machinery. The English court will therefore probably either derive a power to serve the application notice seeking interim relief from its substantive jurisdiction over the parties, or interpret CPR 6.38(1) as implicitly recognizing such a power as regards parties to the proceedings over whom the court has jurisdiction. The latter conclusion is consistent with aspects of the reasoning in *Masri v Consolidated Contractors International Company SAL* [2010] AC 90 (HL), §29. Consequently, it is submitted that the proposition in the original text remains correct, albeit by a different route.

FN 95 second sentence. The revision of CPR Part 6 has abolished the old procedure of imposing a certification of the claimant's grounds of Brussels–Lugano jurisdiction on the claim form, which applied by extension to application notices. The new procedure under new CPR 6.34 and new PD 6B, §2.1 requires filing of a notice on form N510 containing a statement of the grounds of Brussels–Lugano jurisdiction relied on, if the claim form is to be served out of the jurisdiction without permission. However, by reason of the definition of *claim form* in new CPR 6.2(c), this notice procedure will only apply to application notices for interim anti-suit injunctions served before the commencement of proceedings, and not to application notices in proceedings that are already underway, which will apparently require no certification or notice in order to be served out of the jurisdiction on parties to the proceedings. This is workable and indeed logical, since the latter case, the court's jurisdiction against the respondent to the application will already have been invoked on the basis of the CPR 6.34 notice filed together with the claim form.

FN 95 third sentence. The rules on address for service are now contained in new CPR 6.23.

FN 99. See the discussion at Ch 16, §16.12 of this Supplement. **17.47**

The European Court has now held in C-195/07, *Allianz AG v West Tankers Inc (The Front Comor)* [2009] ECR I-66, §§22–23, that an anti-suit injunction to enforce an arbitration clause will fall within the 'arbitration' exception. **17.51**

In the light of the decision in C-195/07, *Allianz AG v West Tankers Inc (The Front Comor)* [2009] ECR I-66, the hypothesis which this paragraph was addressing no longer arises. **17.52**

18

Jurisdiction under the Common Law Rules

A. INTRODUCTION

FN 3. The importance of the traditional touchstone of service under the rules was, however, reaffirmed in *Masri v Consolidated Contractors International (UK) Ltd (No 4)* [2010] 1 AC 90 (HL), §32 (per Lord Mance). **18.02**

B. SERVICE WITHIN THE JURISDICTION

The rules on service were heavily rewritten in the amendments to CPR Part 6 which came into force on 1 October 2009 (pursuant to the Civil Procedure (Amendment) Rules 2008, SI 2008/2178). Service within the jurisdiction is now regulated by CPR Part 6 Sections I to III (Part II dealing with claim forms, and Part III dealing with other documents). **18.04**

FN 7. Service within the jurisdiction at the defendant's residence is now regulated by CPR 6.3(1) and 6.9. The principle set out in *City & Country Properties Ltd v Kamali* [2007] 1 WLR 1219 (CA) should still apply.

FN 8. The Companies Act 2006 is now fully in force.

FN 9. Personal service is now regulated by CPR 6.3(1)(a) and 6.5.

FN 10. Service on defined addresses is now regulated by CPR 6.3(1)(b) to (e) and 6.9, as well as under the Companies Acts.

FN 11. Service on the defendant's agent in the jurisdiction is now regulated by CPR 6.7 and 6.12.

FN 13. Service by an alternative method is now regulated by CPR 6.15.

FN 14. Dispensing with service is now regulated by CPR 6.16.

D. SERVICE OUT OF THE JURISDICTION

18.09 The 'common law' rules on service out of the jurisdiction, once considered of sufficient importance to require direct primary legislation in the Common Law Procedure Act 1852, have come down in the world. Having spent an intermediary century as Rules of Court (first Order XI of the Rules of the Supreme Court, and then CPR 6.20), they are now framed by CPR 6.36 and 6.37 but in reality contained in CPR Part 6 Practice Direction B, paragraph 3.1.

The constitutional implications of permitting the Court's extraterritorial jurisdiction to be regulated by a mere Practice Direction appear not to have been taken seriously. Compared to this, it is perhaps a minor complaint that for the practising litigator, 'Practice Direction 6B, paragraph 3.1(3)' is distinctly unwieldy to pronounce.

See also the hostility to this change expressed by A Dickinson, 'Restrained No More? Service out of the Jurisdiction in the 21st Century' [2010] LMCLQ 1, 12–13.

18.10 FNs 21 and 22. See now CPR 6.37.

E. THE NATURE OF ANTI-SUIT INJUNCTIONS AND CPR 6.20

18.12 CPR 6.20 is now replaced by CPR 6.36 and PD 6B, §3.1.

FN 27. It is submitted that the arguments in the second paragraph of the footnote apply with equal force under the new wording of CPR Part 6.

18.13 CPR 6.20 is now replaced by CPR 6.36 and PD 6B, §3.1.

FN 30. CPR 6.20(3) is now PD 6B, §3.1(3).

CPR 6.20 is now replaced by CPR 6.36 and PD 6B, §3.1. **18.14–18.15**

F. THE HEADS OF JURISDICTION UNDER CPR 6.20

The new wording of CPR Part 6.36 and PD 6B contains a very similar, but not quite identical, list of gateways. **18.16**

The heads of jurisdiction which, now, are those of real practical use for anti-suit injunctions, are PD 6B, §§3.1(1), 3.1(3) and 3.1(6), plus possibly also §3.1(20)—see comments below.

CPR 6.20(4) is now PD 6B, §3.1(5). **18.17**

Old CPR 6.20(1) is now PD 6B, §3.1(1). **18.18**

Old CPR 6.20(2) is now PD 6B, §3.1(2). **18.19**

Old CPR 6.20(3) is now PD 6B, §3.1(3). **18.22**

In *Belletti v Morici* [2009] ILPr 57, §§36–38, Flaux J held that PD 6B, §3.1(3) could only apply where the substantive dispute is before the English courts. However, for this purpose a substantive claim for a final anti-suit injunction would suffice.

Old CPR 6.20(3A) has become PD 6B, §3.1(4). However, the wording of this provision has changed. Old CPR 6.20(3A) provided that permission to serve out could be granted where 'a claim is a part 20 claim and the person to be served is a necessary or property party to the claim against the part 20 claimant'. The new wording allows for permission to serve out where 'a claim is an additional claim under Part 20 and the person to be served is a necessary or proper party to the claim or additional claim'. The former provision could be applied with a degree of precision, even if its rationale was somewhat mysterious. This is simply mystifying. Although the general intent to permit the bringing of appropriate defendants to Additional Claims before the English courts is clear, it is difficult to give precise sense to the exact words used (what is the 'claim' in question? Is it the original claim against the additional claimant? And how can you be a 'necessary and proper party' to your own additional claim?). On its literal wording, this head of jurisdiction could, in theory, afford a broad scope of jurisdiction to anti-suit injunctions, if and to the extent that they could be framed as Additional Claims under CPR Part 20. But anti-suit injunctions rarely, if ever, are framed as Additional Claims. So the tricky task of working **18.23** out precisely how this provision is meant to work can fortunately be left to others.

18.24–18.28 Old CPR 6.20(5) has become PD 6B, §3.1(6).

18.26 FN 55. In *AES UST-Kamenogorsk Hydropower Plant LLP v UST-Kamenogorsk Hydropower Plant JSC* [2010] EHC 772, §25, Burton J reached the contrary conclusion *obiter*: see §§18.40–18.41 of this Supplement below.

18.27 Recent jurisprudence has confirmed that old CPR 6.20(6), now PD 6B, §3.1(6), is sufficiently broad enough to cover quasi-contractual anti-suit injunctions, by which X seeks to force Z, who alleges he has contractual rights against X derived from a contract between X and Y (for example as assignee), to respect an English exclusive forum clause in the contract between X and Y, provided that the terms of that contract satisfy §3.1(6). In *Greene Wood & McClean v Templeton Insurance Ltd* [2009] 1 WLR 2013 (CA), §§16–19, the Court of Appeal held that in order for a claim to be 'in respect of a contract' within the rule, it did not have to be 'in respect of a contract between the intended claimant and the intended defendant'. It was sufficient if the claim 'has a connection with a contract governed by English law'. The looseness of particular connections would be relevant only when assessing whether England was the proper place for a claim. This is a somewhat surprising decision, and could open the door for an unjustifiably wide ambit to the jurisdiction of the court. But the process of narrowing it has already begun. In *Cecil v Bayat* [2010] EWHC 641, §§43-49, Hamblen J restricted this approach by holding that a 'legal' and not merely a 'factual' connection with the relevant contract is required. He defined a legal connection as being where the contract 'needs to be referred to and relied upon to assert the relevant cause of action'. It is as yet unclear whether this elegant approach will stick. But even on this narrowed basis, the doctrine of 'connection' will still easily be broad enough to include quasi-contractual injunctions of this kind.

For critical commentary on *Greene Wood* see A Dickinson, 'Restrained No More? Service out of the Jurisdiction in the 21st Century' [2010] LMCLQ 1.

18.28 In the light of *Greene Wood & McClean v Templeton Insurance Ltd* [2009] 1 WLR 2013 (CA), and *Cecil v Bayat* [2010] EWHC 641, discussed above, it seems clear that, as matters stand *Starlight Shipping Co v Tai Ping Insurance Co Ltd (The Alexandros T)* [2008] 1 Lloyds Rep 230 was wrongly decided on this point.

18.29 The correctness of *Albon v Naza Motor Trading Sdn Bhd (No 4)* [2007] 2 Lloyds Rep 420, §20 on this point remains uncertain. On the one hand, in *Greene Wood & McClean v Templeton Insurance Ltd* [2009] 1 WLR 2013 (CA), the Court of Appeal (to whom *Albon* was cited) adopted a very similar test to Lightman J's test in *Albon*. But on the other hand, the Court of Appeal in *Greene Wood* did not expressly approve the decision in *Albon*. Further, if Hamblen J's narrowing of the test in *Cecil v Bayat* [2010] EWHC 641, §§43–49, establishes itself as the law, it will be arguable that this situation (where a 'vexation'-based anti-suit injunction is sought to enforce a contract governed by English law but without an English exclusive forum clause) does not fall within the 'connection' test derived from *Greene Wood*, because the existence of the contract is merely part of the factual background: the cause of action for the anti-suit injunction depends on principles of equity, and in particular whether the foreign litigation is vexatious and oppressive, and not on any contractual obligation.

Old CPR 6.20(6) is now PD 6B, §3.1(7), and old CPR 6.20(7) is now PD 6B, §3.1(8). **18.30**

Old CPR 6.20(8) is now PD 6B, §3.1(9). **18.32**

FN 64: see now *Kallang Shipping SA Panama v Axa Assurances Senegal (The Kallang) (No 2)* [2009] 1 Lloyds Rep 124; and *Sotrade Denizcilik Sanayi Ve Ticaret AS v Amadou Lo (The Duden)* [2009] 1 Lloyds Rep 145, §§65–68, which are discussed at §3.08 of this Supplement.

FN 67. The matter later proceeded to trial: *Kallang Shipping SA Panama v Axa Assurances Senegal (The Kallang) (No 2)* [2009] 1 Lloyds Rep 124. **18.33**

Old CPR 6.20(11) is now PD 6B, §3.1(12). It should be noted that this provision only permits jurisdiction to be obtained over the trustee of the relevant trust and not over other parties. **18.34**

A significant change has been held to have occurred in relation to what used to CPR 6.20(18). The former wording of this provision was that 'a claim form can be served out of the jurisdiction with the permission of the court if . . . (18) a claim is made under an enactment specified in the relevant practice direction.' **18.35**

Old CPR 6 PD B as it then was listed at §5.2 the following enactments: (1) The Nuclear Installations Act 1965; (2) The Social Security Contributions and Benefits Act 1992; (3) The Directive of the Council of the European Communities dated 15 March 1976 No 76/308/EEC, where service is to be effected in a Member State of the European Union; The Drug Trafficking Offences Act 1994; . . . (7) Part VI of the Criminal Justice Act 1988; (8) The Inheritance (Provision for Family and Dependants) Act 1975; (9) Part II of the Immigration and Asylum Act 1999; (10) Schedule 2 to the Immigration Act 1971; (11) The Financial Services and Markets Act 2000; (12) The Pensions Act 1995; (13) the Pensions Act 2004.

These provisions were the replacements for RSC Order 11(1)(o)–(s) and (u), which similarly permitted service out of the jurisdiction in respect of claims brought under a number of specific statutes.

New PD 6B, §3.1(20) however, provides that:

> a claim form can be served out of the jurisdiction with the permission of the court if . . . (20) A claim is made: (a) under an enactment which allows proceedings to be brought and those proceedings are not covered by any of the other grounds referred to in this paragraph; or (b) under the Directive of the Council of the European Communities dated 15 March 1976 No 76/308/EEC, where service is to be effected in a Member State of the European Union.

(This Directive is a specialist interest: it covers 'mutual assistance for the recovery of claims resulting from operations forming part of the system of financing the European Guidance and Guarantee Fund, and of agricultural levies and customs duties'.)

In *AES UST-Kamenogorsk Hydropower Plant LLP v UST-Kamenogorsk Hydropower Plant JSC* [2010] EWHC 772 (Comm), §24, Burton J, *obiter*, said that he would have been prepared to conclude that an injunction sought to enforce an English arbitration clause under section 37(1) of the Supreme Court Act 1981 could be served out of the jurisdiction under PD 6B, §3.1(20). He rejected the argument that §3.1(20), like its ancestors, was restricted to claims under certain specific statutes.

This cannot be right. First of all, in the specific case with which Burton J was concerned, namely injunctions to enforce a contractual arbitration clause, the proceedings plainly *are* 'covered by' one of 'the other grounds referred to in this paragraph', namely either the contract head in §3.1(6), or the injunction head in §3.1(2). Alternatively, they will at least be covered by their own specific head in the arbitration practice direction, namely CPR 62.5 (depending on whether this is seen as exclusive or not, as to which see §§18.40–18.42 below), in which case §3.1(20) should probably not apply, by extension. Second, it is very unlikely that the draftsmen intended to create a general power to serve out of the jurisdiction any and all injunctions under section 37 of the Supreme Court Act 1981. This would reverse the decision of the House of Lords in *Siskina (Owners of cargo lately laden on board) v Distos Compania Naviera SA (The Siskina)* [1979] AC 210 (HL). Third, it is more likely that §3.1(20) was intended to continue the policy of its predecessors, namely to permit service out of the jurisdiction of proceedings brought under specific statutes dealing with specialist subject matters, that might otherwise not be easy to bring within the remainder of §3.1, whose heads are focussed on the causes of action in play in general civil litigation. Its novelty was solely that by eschewing detailed listing, it aimed to create greater flexibility, and to spare the Rules

Committee the task of exhaustive listing and frequent updating. But it was not intended to create a general power to serve out in respect of any claim which may be made under section 37(1): this is a central part of general civil litigation and service out of claims made under it has always been, and should remain, regulated specifically and in detail by the primary heads of PD 6B, §§3.1(1) to (16).

G. JURISDICTION BY WAY OF COUNTERCLAIM

CPR 6.20 is now replaced by CPR 6.36 and PD 6B, §3.1. The rules requiring a party to give an address for service are now contained in CPR 6.23. **18.36**

FN 72. The CPR references should now be to PD 7A, §3.1 and Form N1; and PD 8A, §2.2 and Form N208.

H. DISCRETION UNDER CPR 6.20

CPR 6.20 is now replaced by CPR 6.36 and PD 6B, §3.1. **18.37–18.39**

I. ARBITRATION CLAIMS

In *AES UST-Kamenogorsk Hydropower Plant LLP v UST-Kamenogorsk Hydropower Plant JSC* [2010] EWHC 772 (Comm), §§18(vii)–(viii); 19(vii), 22, the injunction claimant wished to prevent the injunction defendant from litigating otherwise than in London arbitration, as provided by the arbitration agreement, but did not wish itself actually to commence arbitration proceedings. The injunction defendant challenged the Court's powers to grant permission to service of the proceedings out of the jurisdiction, arguing that even if the proceedings had been validly commenced by arbitration claim form (as to which, see Ch 3, §3.14 of this Supplement) CPR 62.5(c) did not apply where the injunction claimant did not actually intend itself to commence arbitration proceedings, because the requirement in rule 62.5(1)(c)(ii) that 'the seat of the arbitration is *or will be* within the jurisdiction' showed that an arbitration had to at least be intended if it had not yet been commenced. This argument was correctly dismissed by Burton J, who concluded that the reference to a seat in rule 62.5(1)(c) was a matter of location only, and did not require that an arbitration was intended or had been commenced. **18.40**

18.41 Contrary to the analysis in the main text, in *AES UST-Kamenogorsk Hydropower Plant LLP v UST-Kamenogorsk Hydropower Plant JSC* [2010] EWHC 772 (Comm), §25, Burton J suggested *obiter* that PD 6B, §3.1(6) (the old CPR 6.20(5)) would probably not apply to applications to enforce an English law arbitration clause, on the basis of the maxim '*generalia specialibus non derogant*' (the general does not form an exception to the specific). But this is one of those cases where Latin is a bad guide to law, and it is suggested that Burton J's conclusion is unnecessary, and unhelpful. PD 6B, §3.1(6) may well be useful in cases where there is difficulty with the technical provisions of the CPR 62.5. From the point of view of comity, the link with England created by an English law arbitration clause should be sufficient to justify service out of the jurisdiction of proceedings to enforce it.

J. JURISDICTION AND INTERIM ANTI-SUIT INJUNCTIONS

18.44 In *Masri v Consolidated Contractors International Company SAL (No 4)* [2010] AC 90 (HL), the House of Lords did not directly consider Lawrence Collins LJ's concept of ancillary jurisdiction, nor did they expressly reject the notion that jurisdiction could be detached from service. But their judgment assumes, and proceeds on the basis that, the Court will only have jurisdiction in respect of foreigners insofar as the statutory rules on service, and in particular the statutory rules on service out of the jurisdiction, give power for service to be effected: see for example §32. In the circumstances, it is unclear whether Lawrence Collins LJ's wider concept of ancillary jurisdiction independent of the service rules can still be the law, except perhaps as a doctrine defining the circumstances in which it can be appropriate to uphold service *within* the jurisdiction of ancillary proceedings on a foreign party (for example at his address for service).

18.45 See generally the analysis at §18.44 above.

FN 90. The suggestion that there might be an inherent jurisdiction to serve out of the jurisdiction ancillary documents in proceedings has been decisively rejected by the House of Lords in *Masri v Consolidated Contractors International Company SAL (No 4)* [2010] AC 90 (HL), §§31–32.

FNs 91 and 92. In *Masri v Consolidated Contractors International Company SAL (No 4)* [2010] AC 90 (HL), §§31–32, the House of Lords proceeded on the basis that jurisdiction in respect of persons abroad was dependent on the scope of the statutory rules as to service out of the jurisdiction.

FN 94. In *Masri v Consolidated Contractors International Company SAL (No 4)* [2010] AC 90 (HL), §32, the House of Lords unhesitatingly affirmed that 'It has long been established that service out of the jurisdiction requires express authorisation either by statute or in the Rules.' **18.46**

FN 96. The history of RSC Order 11, rule 9(4) was discussed by Lord Mance in *Masri v Consolidated Contractors International Company SAL (No 4)* [2010] AC 90 (HL), §§30–34. However, Lord Mance made it clear that the power provided by rule 9(4) had only applied to the service of documents on existing parties to the proceedings: at §§29–35.

The position has now been largely clarified in *Masri v Consolidated Contractors International Company SAL (No 4)* [2010] AC 90 (HL). In the Court of Appeal, Sir Anthony Clarke had held that old CPR 6.30(2) gave an unconstrained power to permit service out of the jurisdiction of ancillary documents in existing proceedings, even as against non-parties (see CA at §§55–67—this case is referred to under the name of *Masri v Toufic Khoury* [2008] EWCA Civ 876 in the main text). However, in the House of Lords, Lord Mance, giving the sole speech, concluded that this could not be correct. Instead (at HL §§28, 29, 36), he upheld Tomlinson J's conclusion in *Vitol SA v Capri Marine Ltd* [2009] Bus LR 271 that old CPR 6.30(2) was 'concerned with' the service of documents on parties to existing proceedings. **18.47–18.52**

The negative import of this decision is clear: old CPR 6.30(2) (and by parity of reasoning, new CPR 6.38(1) which replaces it in similar although not identical terms) does not create a general power to serve ancillary documents on non-parties. To bring a non-party before the court, it is necessary to satisfy one of the primary heads of jurisdiction (then in old CPR 6.20, now in PD 6B, §3.1): see Lord Mance at §§34, 36.

However, what is still not entirely clear is whether Lord Mance viewed CPR 6.30(2) as creating, or reflecting, a positive power to serve ancillary documents out of the jurisdiction on *parties to the proceedings*. It is submitted that, on the better reading of his judgment, although he has not expressly found this to be so, his reasoning proceeds on the assumption that it is the case. Consequently, the Court of Appeal's conclusion that such an ancillary power exists should be treated as approved, so far as it relates to parties to the proceedings, and has been overruled only so far as it relates to non-parties. Further, where the respondent is within the jurisdiction, including where a party to proceedings has given an address for service, then service can be effected under the rules for service within the jurisdiction.

The result is, as observed in the main text at §18.52, pragmatic. But there remains some uncertainty, because Lord Mance did not expressly find that such a positive power existed. Further, the conceptual basis of the power to serve out remains unclear (as discussed at §18.52 of the main text). Did the ancillary power come from the exercise of jurisdiction over the defendant by means of the primary heads of jurisdiction, or did it arise from the wording of old CPR 6.30(2)? If the latter (which seems more likely given Lord Mance's approach) how is this reconciled with the literal wording of CPR 6.20(2), which is framed in terms of a requirement, rather than the creation of a power? In the circumstances, the suggestion in the main text that old CPR 6.30(2), and now new CPR 6.38(1), would benefit from the (further) attention of the Rule Committee remains valid.

An additional factor has been introduced by other aspects of the new wording of CPR Part 6 (which came into force before the debates in their Lordships' House in *Masri (No 4)*, but after the applications with which the appeal before them was concerned, and so was not relevant to the appeal). CPR 6.39 now deals specifically with the service of application notices on a non-party to proceedings. However, this provision can naturally read as permissive only, and not power-creating, and in the light of the House of Lords' reasoning in *Masri*, it is submitted that it will not be read as positively creating an unconstrained power to serve proceedings on non-parties independent of the primary jurisdictional heads in CPR 6.36 and PD 6B, §3.1. This is confirmed by CPR 6.2(c) which states that 'claim' includes 'any application made before action or to commence proceedings', and thus demonstrates that the primary jurisdictional heads, which formally apply to claim forms, are also intended to cover applications against non parties.

18.47 FN 98. Old CPR 6.30(2) is now new CPR 6.38(1). The decision in *Vitol SA v Capri Marine Ltd* [2009] Bus LR 271 has now been upheld by the House of Lords in *Masri v Consolidated Contractors International Company SAL (No 4)* [2010] AC 90 (HL).

FN 99. In the light of the House of Lords' decision in *Masri v Consolidated Contractors International Company SAL (No 4)* [2010] AC 90 (HL), it now appears possible to serve an application notice on parties to the proceedings under CPR 6.38(1) (replacing CPR 6.30(2)). However, non-parties must be served under the primary heads of jurisdiction. Consequently, the decision in *C Inc Plc v L* [2001] 2 Lloyds Rep 459 has partially been rehabilitated, and the Court of Appeal's decision in *Masri v Khoury* (also now reported as part of *Masri v Consolidated Contractors International Company SAL (No 4)* [2010] AC 90) has partially been overruled.

FN 100. Old CPR 6.20(4) is now PD 6B, §3.1(5). In *Belletti v Morici* [2009] ILPr 57, §§3, 9, 3 it was confirmed that PD 6B, §3.1(5) is the sole and exclusive head for the service out of the jurisdiction of applications under section 25(1) of the Civil Jurisdiction and Judgments Act 1982.

FN 102. The requirement of an address for service is now contained in new CPR 6.23.

For discussion of the decision(s) in the *Masri* litigation, see A Briggs, 'Enforcing and reinforcing an English judgment' [2008] LMCLQ 421. **18.49**

FN 107. In *Masri v Consolidated Contractors International Company SAL (No 4)* [2010] AC 90 (HL), §32, Lord Mance confirmed that the identification of a primary head of jurisdiction would be necessary against a non-party. But as against an existing party, it appears that old CPR 6.30(2) (new CPR 6.38(1)) may suffice. **18.51**

Old CPR 6.20 is now replaced by new CPR 6.36 and PD 6B, §3.1. **18.53**

Service of applications for interim relief within the jurisdiction is now governed by a new set of rules in new CPR 6 Part III. **18.56**

The wording of CPR Part 6 has been heavily rewritten in this regard. Nevertheless, it is submitted that the same substantive result should follow. In the light of the decision of the House of Lords in *Masri v Consolidated Contractors International Company SAL (No 4)* [2010] AC 90 (HL), it appears to be the case that interim applications against parties to the proceedings can be justified under new CPR 6.38(1), and thus the use of the primary heads of CPR 6.36 and PD 6B, §3.1 will be unnecessary for the most part. But in relation to non-parties, it will remain the case that the applicant can and must serve his application out of the jurisdiction by bringing it within the primary heads of jurisdiction. This is possible because although CPR 6.36 provides powers in respect of the service out of the jurisdiction of the 'claim form', CPR 6.2(c) defines claim to include application notices in 'any application made before action or to commence proceedings.' **18.57**

Old CPR 6 Part III is now new CPR 6 Part IV. Old CPR 6.20(3) is now new PD 6B, §3.1(3).

FN 121. For analysis, see text of §18.57 above. The definition of 'claim' and 'claim form' and 'application' and 'application notice' in old CPR 6.18 is now replaced by CPR 6.2(c), in somewhat different terms.

In *Belletti v Morici* [2009] 2 CLR 525, §§3, 9, 3 it was confirmed that PD 6B, §3.1(5) is the sole and exclusive head for the service out of the jurisdiction **18.59** of applications under section 25(1) of the Civil Jurisdiction and Judgments Act 1982.

18.61 In relation to the exclusivity of CPR 62.5, see *AES UST-Kamenogorsk Hydropower Plant LLP v UST-Kamenogorsk Hydropower Plant JSC* [2010] EWHC 772 (Comm), and the discussion at §18.40–18.41 above.

Appendix: Precedents

B. APPLICATION FOR AN INTERIM INJUNCTION WITH NOTICE

(B1) Application Notice

Form N244(CC) for Commercial Court applications is no longer on the HMCS website, which only has the standard form application notice N244, which has a rather different format. However, N244(CC) appears still to be in use in practice. Either is likely to be acceptable in the Commercial Court.

(B2) Draft Order

Notes (7) The '*Krgyz*' approach of awarding indemnity costs against an injunction defendant against whom a contractual anti-suit injunction has been granted, on the grounds of his breach of the exclusive forum clause, was also adopted in *A v B (No 2)* [2007] 2 CLC 203.

However, in *C v D* [2008] 1 Lloyds Rep 239 (CA), §33, the Court of Appeal declined to extend this approach. There were a number of grounds of distinction. First, no proceedings had actually been started abroad. Second, the Court of Appeal had justified the injunction on the grounds that the parties had impliedly agreed that all supervisory proceedings in respect of an arbitration should be brought before the courts of the seat of the arbitration (§16). But since the basis for the injunction was an implied agreement only, when it came to costs, the Court of Appeal considered that the basis for the injunction was only 'analogous' to an exclusive jurisdiction clause, and that this analogy was too thin a basis to justify the extension of any principle that indemnity costs should be awarded (even if such a principle should indeed be applied in cases where an actual exclusive jurisdiction clause was breached, a point which the Court of Appeal left open). Third, the Court of Appeal concluded that indemnity costs should not be awarded because the question of contractual incorporation which had been debated was on one which 'conflicting views should legitimately be held.' It is submitted that this third ground of distinction should be of general application, so that the *Krgyz* approach should be applicable only in plain cases of breach.

In addition, the Court of Appeal deliberately declined to endorse the *Krygz* line of authorities even in such cases as they might apply. It is submitted, as observed in the main text, that this cautious approach was wise: the award of indemnity costs should in most cases follow from conduct in litigation, not the merits of the underlying case; and the mechanical award of indemnity costs because it has been found that an exclusive jurisdiction clause has been breached is not an appropriate approach to the exercise of the court's discretion on costs.

C. APPLICATION FOR AN INTERIM INJUNCTION WITHOUT NOTICE

(C3) Witness Evidence in Support

§20 CPR 6.20(5)(d) is now new CPR Part 6 PD B, §3.1(6)(d).

Notes (6) CPR 6.20 and 6.21 are now replaced by new CPR 6.36–6.37 and new CPR Part 6 PD B, §3.1.

Index